THE GROWTH OF TRUTH

THE GROWTH OF TRUTH

A True Story of the Heaven and Hell of a Psychic Medium

By Debbie Raymond-Pinet and Bonnie Meroth

Copyright © 2012 by Debbie Raymond-Pinet and Bonnie Meroth.

ISBN: Softcover   978-1-4691-8779-2
          Ebook   978-1-4691-8780-8

All rights reserved. No part of this book may be reproduced or transmitted in any form or by any means, electronic or mechanical, including photocopying, recording, or by any information storage and retrieval system, without permission in writing from the copyright owner.

Cover photo Cloud Elephants

This book was printed in the United States of America.

To order additional copies of this book, contact:
Xlibris Corporation
1-888-795-4274
www.Xlibris.com
Orders@Xlibris.com
112474

This book is the true story of a psychic medium.
Any blatant resemblance to a living person is coincidence.
Any blatant resemblance to the dead is insignificant.

Note to Reader:

Debbie Raymond-Pinet is absolutely the real thing.

In the past, my experience with mediums has been limited to the twenty times I saw Whoopi Goldberg in the movie *Ghost*.

Now, I know there is no limit to my experiences.

Bonnie Meroth

TABLE OF CONTENTS

Prologue xiii
Part One: The Beginning 1
Part Two: Evil 15
Part Three: Something Better 61
Part Four: Truth in Knowledge 89
Part Five: The Past 107
Part Six: The Future 119
Addendum 149
Afterword 151
Acknowledgements 153

*Some feelings are to mortals given
With less of earth in them than heaven:*

Sir Walter Scott: Lady of the Lake

*Millions of spiritual creatures walk the earth
Unseen, both when we wake and when we sleep.*

Milton: Paradise Lost

PROLOGUE

Suddenly blinded by a brilliant light, I saw and felt huge purple-framed white wings wrap around me a split second before I heard the explosive boom. Just as fast, the shimmering wings released me and the bright radiance disappeared.

The smell of burned rubber and leaking oil permeated the car and assaulted my nostrils. Still gripping the steering wheel, I stared through the broken windshield feeling the frigid winter temperature bite my face and I realized another vehicle had hit me full-force and head-on.

I gave thanks three times for not being killed.

Completely unharmed, I stepped out of a total rumpled heap of metal to the face of the driver of the truck that had hit me.

No one stopped to help and I was no where near Heaven, but I had seen the sight of it under the wings of an angel.

And, I had also seen the truth about my life.

PART ONE
THE BEGINNING

*All we know
Of what they do above,
Is that they happy are,
And that they love.*

Edmund Waller: 1645

CHAPTER 1

It started with Bobby in the late summer of 1974.

I was 2 years old.

The first time it happened was when I was playing at the kitchen table with the bathtub that went with my favorite doll. I felt a tugging at my earlobe, but when I turned around, I saw no one. Then, the bubbles in the little plastic tub dissipated as though someone behind me had blown them away.

Again, no one was there.

Suddenly, as if appearing out of air, I saw him walking into another room. He was around the age of seven, blonde and blue-eyed and totally unfamiliar.

And, he was deathly pale.

I scooted after him but he was no where to be seen. I remember looking under the bathrobe that was always hanging on a hook in the bedroom and I looked in other places, but I just could not find him. Like a normal toddler, I was confused and, like a normal toddler, I quickly forgot and went on to other things.

Over the months, I would frequently feel someone tugging at my ear or pulling at my blankets at night. I would see him from time to time and he would tease me like a brother would a little sister. I knew he meant no harm. No one else ever saw him, yet he was there when I was at the lake or went to the store. Sometimes, he would just wait for me at home in our spooky basement stairwell.

Around the age of four, I realized he was dead.

CHAPTER 2

I probably should have guessed it sooner. Everyone said I was precocious from the time I was a toddler and I was--about worldly things. No one knew I was worldly about ghostly things. I knew no one else saw Bobby. I knew his name, but nobody ever greeted him when he came through the door and he never needed a bath like I would after a long hot summer day. He never had a plate at dinner and he was never involved in our daily prayers. He did not eat but, strangely enough, he would comment on food and admit he missed his mother's chocolate chip cookies.

I was always the one to keep the conversation going with Bobby because words didn't come easily for him for some reason. Although young, I came to know for certain that I was the only one who witnessed this miracle of life after death so Bobby and I developed our unique friendship basically all by ourselves. People thought he was my imaginary playmate.

As time went on, Bobby seemed to become stronger in his world with the stuff he could do. He moved himself quickly from place to place. The first time he walked through a wall I thought it was really cool until I tried it myself and, of course, failed miserably, but I did experience something else.

I put my two tiny hands on the vanilla colored satin wallpaper, stepped closer and flattened my cheek against the wall. Feeling a warm tingly sensation traveling up my arms to my head, I closed my eyes, and sensed Bobby was there but could not apprehend where he was or how he got there. In my mind's eye, he was clearly in the next room. I ran into the room to see him and sure enough, there he was kneeling next to a big toy truck he loved. As I knelt with him, I never asked how he did the things he did, but I was in awe of his magic and I wished I could go with him through any wall.

He hardly spoke and always seemed sad, but I kept him busy with imagination hide-and-seek, one of our favorite games. Because he could pass through walls and I could not, it was not easy catching him and when I did tag Bobby, my fingers went right through his skin. Some days I could see him clearly and other times he would be very faint. It reminded me of how batteries would run out in toys. I knew his batteries needed recharging when he was transparent, but I didn't know how he accomplished that.

I was too little.

After spending hours with Bobby, I was moody and exhausted, not a typical thing for me to be. Like a normal child, I would fight the feelings by escaping to a bedroom television where, lying on a quilted comforter and immersed in the screen, I recharged my batteries like Bobby somehow recharged his.

CHAPTER 3

When I was seven, I had a friend, Lance, who lived next door. He was alive. He was also seven like I was and he became my neighborhood playmate. For some reason, that's when all hell broke loose. The floodgates of my psychic abilities opened and Bobby really started to talk to me. I could hear him clearly saying things like he missed his mother. He also told me he would no longer be my friend if I continued my relationship with my live buddy. He was jealous and I found it strange because the two boys had so much in common.

Obviously, Bobby could not see that he was much like my earthly friend and my earthly friend could not see Bobby, of course, so he was clueless. They were the same age and looked alike with blonde hair and blue eyes. They even had common mannerisms like kicking rocks while we walked.

When I finally confessed to the boy next door that I could see a ghost, it didn't go as well as I had hoped. I was in his backyard hanging upside down on the monkey bars with my hair messed up and covering my face. I tried to explain to him who Bobby was and asked if he would let Bobby play with us. Scared to death, he blurted "no" and ran to into the house.

I did not see him for five days. In my young, unworldly innocence and simplicity, I just figured if I told him about Bobby, we could all play together. I thought it was ridiculous to lose a friendship with either one of them over something I considered nothing. Obviously, my neighborhood boy did not. He avoided my phone calls and me tapping on his window to come out and play every day. He never even glanced out his window.

On the sixth day, and with the proud determination of a precocious 7-year-old and also with a sick stomach, I decided to head to his house. I banged on the door and called his name. Seconds passed before he opened the door a few inches.

"Hi," I said resolutely.

He stared in astonishment while looking around as if he were looking for my ghostly friend.

"Want to come out and play? We're making water balloons."

"Is he with you? You know, Bobby?" he asked uncomfortably with the same degree of fear he had nearly a week before.

I looked into the hallway and saw my other friend standing in the corner.

"Yup. He's standing right there." My right finger pointed to the corner.

"What's he doing there?"

"He's waiting for you to finish being stupid and come outside and throw water balloons," I said rather irreverently.

He slammed the door and I sat on the steps with the expectation that he would reconsider and play with Bobby and me. A few minutes passed and out he came with sneakers in hand. Off we went to my house to get soaked with water balloons.

That was the last time. He never did play with Bobby and me again. I just assumed he would join us during the long summer after that wonderful day, but it never happened.

Bobby was pleased to have me all to himself. That was fine by me because whenever I would bring anyone else into the mix, it never worked out. I decided it would be better to keep my secrets and be his friend forever.

Bobby was my first ghost, but he sure wasn't my last.

That autumn was when I started to clearly hear other ghosts, too.

CHAPTER 4

I had not seen Bobby for awhile when he suddenly showed up out of the blue one early fall day. I asked him where he had been.

"Everywhere," he said and with the one word, he popped close to my bed and then popped to the window to view a dog outside.

"What do you mean 'everywhere'? "

I had been concerned for weeks because I had not seen him and he was usually around at least every couple of days.

Jumping out of bed, I put socks on my cold feet.

"I've been with a gentleman. He teaches me all kinds of stuff and how to do stuff better, like moving things."

With that gesture, he looked at a spoon on the bureau. Just by pointing, he pushed it an inch and the spoon rotated slowly. I was impressed.

"I can yell louder now too, and I even rode a horse in a desert."

With a jump, he landed on my bed and lay down as if he were exhausted. Legs crossed and arms behind his head, he watched me do my morning chores and prepare for school by gathering papers and books and packing my peanut butter and marshmallow sandwich into a brown bag,

He wanted to go to school with me and I said it would be fine if he did not bug me. I explained my busy schedule for the day and that I had to be focused and he agreed to not be distracting if I let him tag along.

I really HAD to pay attention in class.

But, I had not forgotten about the "gentlemen" and if I pressed Bobby further about him, Bobby might be upset enough to disappear for another long length of time. I did tip toe around questions, carefully asking about the gentleman. Mostly, I wanted to know who else could see Bobby.

"Who is this 'gentleman' you told me about and why do you call him that?" I asked casually.

"He introduced himself as "Gentleman" so I think that's his name. I also see others call him that," Bobby said nonchalantly as he kicked a rock that landed at least ten feet in front of us.

I looked around and was thankful that no one noticed.

"Can he see you? I mean, like I see you?"

Selfish or not, I really wanted to know.

Puzzled, he replied, "Of course he can see me. He's exactly like me. Not you."

With a see-you-later gesture, he walked through a wall and left me as I took my seat in the classroom, but his words haunted me over and over. The gentleman was dead, but I had not seen him.

The school day dragged until I could finally head up the hill to the baseball field where I daily walked with Bobby. I noticed a wizened old man I had never seen before standing at the top. Avoiding him, I kept my head down looking at the lush green grass passing under my sneakers while casting furtive glances back to see if he still stood there. The third time I looked, he was gone.

Uneasy, I started to run home, picking up pencils that bounced from my bag. Suddenly, the old man with ghostly eyes in a face like a wrinkled prune appeared in front of me. Dismissing any thought of losing pencils, I ran as fast as I could looking back to see him wave to me with his left hand. Then, he disappeared.

Shocked and in disbelief at seeing an adult spirit, not one my age, I made it home and slammed the door behind me. I knew I had seen a ghost, but not like Bobby and my mind screamed at seeing another one. Then I realized there were so many dead people, it was unrealistic to assume Bobby would be the only one. However, this one scared me because he was not a kid my age. He was not a kid like me. He was elderly and did not talk. I could see him and he knew how to adroitly pop in and out to various locations like Bobby did, but innately, I knew he was different.

Foolishly, I blocked the door to my bedroom with my bag and jumped under the blankets hoping never to see him again. I prayed the Our Father and Hail Mary several times the way I learned in church school. I knew that we should pray and allow God in our lives and God would save us from our ailments, fear, addictions and abuse.

And, maybe He would save me from ghosts.

With no one around to hear but my stuffed giraffe, I wondered if God COULD protect me from ghosts. They had not been on the list of saves.

I was an 8-year-old who could see dead people when no one else could. Sobbing with my prayers, I shared my fear and grief with God then fell into an exhausted sleep until my head started to tingle.

It tingled in a nice way like excitement in anticipation of something good about to happen. Like happy butterflies in the tummy at Christmas time. Thoughts bounced everywhere through my head and then a small breeze lifted me a few inches off the bed. Transparent, I was standing next to my body while a white light glimmered from the left. I looked down at myself lying shimmering in a beautiful glow. Calm totally enveloped me. I asked no questions, but saw many wings and faces staring as I stared back. I felt deep, profound and unconditional love and understanding. I watched my sleeping body float effortlessly above the mattress surrounded by winged figures. I was totally under the security of their wings.

I watched for what seemed like forever. Eventually, the brightness and spirits left the bedroom. The breeze stopped. There was nothingness. I lay back down into my body knowing and accepting the answers. I was too young to put a name to it, but I finally understood who or what I was and I was okay with it.

CHAPTER 5

Bobby went through the same physical changes as I did growing up and we both turned ten with long legs, higher cheekbones and longer hair. I would have a hair cut and suddenly his would be shorter. I physically matured. He physically matured. I didn't understand why, but he grew with me. It seemed magical that he could do all that even if he were dead.

To me, he was a normal kid doing normal things like attending class, enjoying softball and the new MTV with its array of videos. He was flamboyant, moody and really articulate in communication and with our imaginary play and even music. He was experiencing what my live friends and I were going through.

Sometimes being dead didn't seem to bother Bobby. Lance just didn't get it. That was normal. Bobby understood exactly where he was and exactly where I was.

I often pondered what it would be like to be Bobby and he shared the same thoughts about what it would be like to be me.

We would sit in the basement closet on the black trash bags full of old clothing that, in spite of the plastic, felt as comfortable as a down blanket to me. It became our favorite place and my soft place to fall when things were too much to handle. I felt secure there and I was confident enough to share with him that I wanted to be able to go through walls and do all the stuff he could. He told me that there were times he was afraid and that he just wanted to walk into his front door and see his mother again like he did when he was alive.

Undisturbed in our closet, we cherished our alone time. Bobby would take me to imaginative beautiful places that only we could know. An open field or grassy hill filled with birds and the sounds of nature would be the backdrop for us as we played. We spent fun time together and laughed, holding hands as we climbed to the top of the knoll and looked down in amazement at the entire world at our feet. At least it seemed like the entire world. I could feel infinity and sometimes fear of what I could experience with what I now considered my gift—the ability to "be" with a ghost.

When I was older, I understood the symbolism of all the climbing of hills. They were difficulties to overcome in physical life but as a child, with nothing but the sound of peace and the sun beating down on our arms, we enjoyed the heaven he so carefully presented to me.

Bobby had a huge responsibility showing me his world and protecting me from harm at the same time. I never realized how much he did protect me until once in the closet without Bobby, I left this world by myself and went to the cushiony grass I often shared with him. I felt the familiar pleasant tingle without Bobby in my subconscious vision. Scared, I jumped up and visualized home. Running toward my house, in panic and with difficulty breathing, I fell to the ground with my head to my chest sobbing. It was the first time I was alone in Bobby's world and I was lost. I didn't know how to return to our closet. The panic ruled me until I felt the plastic of those bags give against the back of my sweaty legs.

Tears of relief spilled down my cheeks because I was in the physical world, but Bobby was not there. I had no idea why. As I opened the door to leave the closet, I realized it was six o'clock at night. The afternoon had passed while I had gone to another place and had come back to find my way to the reality of home with the smell of potatoes and liver for supper. And, I did it all by myself.

I went into the bathroom and splashed cold water over my face drying off with the fragrant brown butterfly towel that always hung on the chrome bar. When I glanced up to the mirror over the sink, I saw the hill we ran up and heard the birds sing and rustle of leaves that were in Bobby's heaven. I was wide awake. The scene was enough confirmation that I had not been tricked by my imagination.

What I had been through was real, not the games played by an over imaginative child. The pleasant trip was not a dream from a nap. I was relieved that I really did it, but scared to death and I knew no one would believe me. I wanted to go back to that place of peace and nature. Little did I know that the place was not all for the good. It was in that place where I learned how Bobby died.

PART TWO
EVIL

"Evil springs up, and flowers, and bears no seed,
And feeds the green earth with its swift decay,
Leaving it richer for the growth of truth."

James Russell Lowell: Prometheus

CHAPTER 6

Bobby continued to teach me to have the visions as we sat in our place in the closet. I learned to relax my mind and to focus. The visions materialized easier and clearer even in unfamiliar locales. One afternoon, he showed me a 7-year-old blonde boy who was walking ahead of me with a baseball bat and leather glove hanging over his shoulder. It was hot and he wore only a dirty white t-shirt and blue jean shorts. His left sneaker was untied and he looked like a typical kid who just left a baseball game with his friends.

Holding his bat tight, he seemed to pick up his pace. I continued to follow and saw the boy look over his shoulder to notice a gray hatchback car idling behind him. As he approached a corner, the boy ran and took a right turn into a dirty alley. I could smell the disgusting odor of trash and feel the sick feeling he had in the pit of his stomach.

Blocking any means of escape, the car followed the boy. A man about six feet tall wearing a red shirt left the vehicle. I noticed his greasy hands and gray curly hair looped around his cap. Swaying, he wore grimy jeans that stunk of dirt and work boots covered with soot. He grabbed the boy.

Boy and man struggled. Panting with fear, the boy let go of his bat and I heard a loud clank as they fell to the ground. I was thinking he should scream, but no sound came out of his mouth. Again, fear overtook him and I knew what was going to happen next. Shivering, he gave in quickly, knees buckling beneath him.

Within seconds, the abuser finished his sexual assault. Intentionally, he slammed the bat into the boy's head with a swift and mortal blow and threw the limp body into the back of the car onto a stained black cover acrid with car oil.

I followed the man home where he had a conversation with his mother.

She never left her chair in the dark living room but asked where he was all day. He answered her with a none-of-your-business tone and jumped into the shower and masturbated. After shaving his face which reflected nothing about what had happened earlier, he got back in his car, drove to a bridge a few miles away and lit up a cigarette.

The open driver's window let in the humidity as he flicked out the cigarette before he tossed the body of my friend, Bobby, into the murky brown waters of the river—the splash of closure in a final testimony to the death of a young boy would not be going home to his mother's chocolate chip cookies.

I saw it all.

I felt it all.

I knew Bobby's relief in knowing that I knew what happened to him. After he showed me his death from the Other Side, he became more out going and positive. I had seen and heard his memory as clear as on the day he was murdered and that sharing with me helped him heal. He trusted me with that knowledge and then he seemed to let go of his sadness and anger.

I knew that vision was the truth and regardless of its intensity and impact on me, it was the catalyst of me feeling the responsibility to help others in the same way by learning how their loved ones died. I thought that maybe it would bring relief to other spirits if they could share what they felt at the time they passed. I could be the one to help them because I was the one who could communicate with them. I could reach them and answer any of their questions so they could find happiness on the Other Side. I could help the ones they left behind.

Sitting still on the plastic bags, I felt excited and anxious thinking this was absolutely absurd and I was not going to do this. I felt I could barely deal with a few spirits let alone talk to ALL of them. What was I thinking? I did not have to think about it. When I opened those receptive thoughts in my mind, a box lid lifted to let in more spirits.

They came piling in.

CHAPTER 7

In an almost hallucinating state, tingling sensations waved a feeling of peace and comfort from my head to my toes. I fell into a heavy sleep and woke up startled by the sound of someone entering my room. Turning slowly, the sound of feet dragging on the carpet made me count starting at one. When I arrived at number eight, the footsteps stopped directly on the side of my bed.

I lay in utmost fright as cold air swept over my rigid face. Lying as flat as I could, I felt a breath on my head traveling down to my neck as a green fog formed with it. Like someone's indistinct face that I could not see, the fog worked its way up from my feet to my head. My lungs could not get enough air.

I felt like I was being crushed by a large stone. I could not move or scream. Over and over in my mind, I recited the Lord's Prayer. By the third time I sent out the prayer, Jesus helped me. I know it was Jesus. The fog lifted off my body and without its weight, I could breathe again. Jumping out of bed, I ran from the room trembling with fear. I spent the rest of the night on the couch in a fetal position.

The next morning I knew I had to confront whatever that fog was and I confided in Bobby, but he had never heard of such a thing and was not interested in knowing. With total indifference, he just kept riding the roller coasters he was on at the time counting how many he could go on without buying a ticket.

What I had seen was not normal for a kid to see or to deal with and I knew all that but, again, I wasn't normal and I knew that, too. I was me—a young girl who could see and communicate with ghosts in every capacity. I had seen haunting movies that were based on the imaginations of film producers, but mine were real.

Every day real.

Me dealing with it was another matter entirely.

The Lord's Prayer helped me out of the last predicament with the green fog, but I had to know if the fog could be harmful and what else could be out there. I needed answers.

Now.

Because Bobby was no help, I started to ask questions to other ghosts. If I brought the questions to anyone around me on earth, they would judge me, so I never did. I was on my own and had to deal with it face to face, mortal to spirit, good to bad.

At this early age, I was learning the difference between bad and good spirits. Bad spirits manifested in a malady. If I felt sick or had a headache, I knew I was around negative ones. Positive spirits would warm me with unconditional love. I set up boundaries or rules on how spirits could cohabitate with me in my world and at the same time, I learned that they were supposed to have their own limitations about manners in their world. They were to respect me as I did them.

By the time I was ten, I realized the importance of privacy because of the changes already starting in my body. I was in puberty. I needed to be alone when I dressed, when I showered. No other soul should be in that shower with me. I just innately knew that any spirit should not enter a physical person's space without permission--just like live people should respect the privacy of others.

If a spirit did not go by the rules, it could not come into my world or my shower. By establishing these parameters, I set limitations on the spirits with whom I would communicate. My mandate lessened the amount of Other Side visitors who came to me out of the blue. My rules worked.

Spirits easily shared their stories with me and I learned of their struggles, death, love and accidents, but none affected me as much as Bobby's murder, maybe because Bobby was the first soul I encountered or maybe he just became the closest. I understood and reciprocated the loss of the other spirits and they would move on. Each ghost shared what they felt would be a heaven to them and I figured out that heaven is what they made it out to be.

"Whatever they wish heaven to be, is what they receive. I feel so happy knowing Jesus created a place for us and that one day I can create my own," I shared with Bobby.

"Yours won't be ready for a long while," he told me. I had no idea what that meant, but I understood it as I would be alive for a very long time.

"I would need what I learned in church as well as some rules to deal with serious issues. Then, I can handle more spirits. I know all about you. My mind is full of stuff and I don't know where I got it. I just know so much I did not know before," I confided to my dear friend on the Other Side. There was much to deal with.

Going through puberty was hard enough and I had to handle that physical and mental maturation as well as a life that no one else knew about. I felt completely alone. But, in fact, I really was not. I had new ghosts every day and now was the time to figure out what the heck I was going to do about it.

CHAPTER 8

My body lay limp on the bed that I once considered a haven from dusk to dawn. Most of the deathly visitors came at night and it sure put a cramp on my sleeping habits. I would not move if I heard any noise and I would keep my eyes closed until I couldn't do so any longer. I was consumed and became frustrated by voices in foreign languages I did not understand.

All the spirits, good and bad, came at especially 3:00 a.m., a time when everyone is vulnerable because of "Dead Time," proven by paranormal investigators as the most active time for spirits. Although I appreciated their stories, I was desperately losing sleep with their presence. Again, I needed to enforce rules and one major rule was to let sleeping humans lie. Of course, not every spirit or spirit villain adhered to it, but enough did so that I recognized a very appreciated night's sleep. My nemesis, evil, was always a horrific ordeal and the game of good and evil continued as my desire to help those on the Other Side escalated and I was truly making a difference.

Evil would remind me of its presence by taking me hostage to a restrictive place of uncertainty and violence as I lay rigid on the bed. I would struggle to breathe and was unable to move or speak, but I could hear a low grumble that intensified the lack of control I had over my body. When this diabolical enemy came, five skeletal figures bound with large chains appeared with buckles held tight to their legs. Staring at me like I was their last meal, they growled and exuded a putrid smell of blood as organs showed through bones and skin adding nausea to my apprehension.

Movements of nothing that seemed like everything to me enveloped my head that felt like it was being squeezed of its contents. I could not scream. I could see my arms and legs bolted to the bed and feel the pain. Emotions of dishonesty, sexual abuse, and substance use filled my head with nightmares. Closing my eyes and praying for relief from this constant assault was my only choice and as if in a dream, I asked for any hierarchy to help. Once again, I was prey to the cobra of fog that entered the room.

Moments later, a cool breeze wisped my long hair away from my face as glittery white winged beings surrounded me forcing screams of skeletal entities to go away in black smoke back through the wall from which they came.

I understood that by focusing on the light that came from my prayers, I could protect myself and they would protect me, but I was still scared to death and crying, I held my blanket tight and they all left me to be in peace. My head felt like a freight train ran over it. I wished for the deep sleep that brought dancing angels dressed in white robes surrounded by vibrant colors and that hint of fragrant roses that was always with them.

I was still questioning why this was happening to me. Only a higher being would know that answer, maybe someone close to God and when I awoke, I went to a church service where I heard the words said by my priest to confirm that I had really and truly witnessed the forces of evil on another level: *"Fear not, to those who have hurt you. Hold them to your heart and forgive them for their selfishness and disobedience. For they know not what they do at that time. It will be up to the Lord, the Highest God, to seek their repent in all of his glory."*

I wondered if the truth of what I was feeling came from me surviving and thus conquering evil and evil would have to deal with God. I wondered if the Lord would be my shepherd and protect me from all things bad so I could continue helping those on the Other Side. I felt courage and strength from that thought and I convinced myself that I could confront anything that haunted me. Being pinned to my bed was no longer acceptable. I had the right to use my gift with spiritual use as the Bible said—an affirmation that would save me from hurt during my life.

This affirmation was confirmed by my priest with whom I had shared my life during confession. He said I had a gift that needed to be accepted without condemnation when I used it, but some people I knew here on earth had a difficult time with this fact.

Some people not here on earth had a difficult time with it, too.

CHAPTER 9

He stood there with his black suit and wide brimmed square top pilgrim hat and stared at me as I sat on the front steps of the porch on an early autumn day. I was near my twelfth birthday. I sneaked glances at him wondering where he came from. His clothes were old-fashioned and not at all contemporary. He was definitely an unhappy person obviously reflected in the face that stared me down. From a distance, he politely tipped his hat to me and then popped away like spirits can do. I glanced around the yard and was relieved he was gone. His presence brought me fear and nausea. I knew he was not a nice guy. At this juncture, I was well able to determine good spirits from bad and I knew he was the latter.

By now, I was in full blown puberty. My breasts were growing and, typical of early teenagers, I carefully hid them with a tank top and short-sleeved shirt. I also hid the fact that I had an unintentional crush on Bobby. He and I were as close as ever. Not only could he do amazing magical things, but he understood me totally. Between hero worship and hormones, I was in love, replete with all the little stomach butterflies. He was more intelligent, more sensitive to me than my peers and he understood me for what I was. To boot, skate boarding was not his primary focus like all the earthly boys.

I would rather have had my ethereal relationship with Bobby than to kiss a real boy or go to a school dance. I loved sharing spiritual things, ideas, thoughts and my visions with him almost daily. By now, I was having teen delusions of grandeur thinking that I must be someone special because of my gift and my ego took over. The negative events were still there, but I had more of a handle on them. They came in threes, so I knew when the bad things would start and when they would end. I could protect myself with a white light shield. I even used holy water. I figured out that something was warning me to stop the work I was doing helping those on the Other Side. I also figured out the bad was constantly on a mission to take down the good.

More so than not, I typically had the ghosts under control, but it sure was difficult shopping or being at a ball game where the ghosts interspersed with the crowds. It was hard to do simple things like picking out a pair of shoes or pitching a softball. I would scrunch myself tighter to make room for the spirits who were thrilled I could see them when I was not thrilled. They would end up taking space between me and the next person. I had to find a place by myself to try to be alone. My walkman was constantly stuck in my ears to let them know I was ignoring them and that I wanted privacy. I honestly thought that if I did that, they would go away.

They did not.

One night I was at a party with lots of people, loud music, drinking and the typical tom foolery that went on at these things. At 8:45 p.m., I had an unforgettable to-this-day living nightmare. I was dribbling a basketball around the driveway hoop and caught the sight of two boys around my age. I stood in horror letting loose of my ball that bounced toward them as they stood there dripping wet. Their skin was all blue. None of us said a word. Shaken from the sight, I ran into the house and peered out the heavy green drapes to see if the boys followed me. Thankfully, they did not come after me.

On the way home, I bit my nails into oblivion. I was semi-aware of familiar sounds and smells surrounding me in the car as I zoned in and out until the hum of the car engine stopped. Too exhausted to shower, I fell into bed in my clothes that smelled of campfire and sweat and I dreamed of the two boys who stared at me with helpless eyes. Still, they spoke nothing. I wakened in a panic and realized I was drooling, but safe. They had come to me even in my sleep. My sub conscious mind had taken over even in my dreams. I fell right back to sleep and waited for the next time I would see the boys because I knew there would be a next time, awake or asleep.

CHAPTER 10

We lived in a three family apartment building and I was allowed to walk freely about the building. Because I was basically a loner, I would sneak up the front stairs to the mudroom and listen to people talk or sit inside and watch speeding cars through the window. I could sit there and, if I wanted, go to my quiet place on the Other Side to the peace and contentment I found there—a happiness that no one knew about and that I could share only with Bobby. Or, I could visit my grandmother who lived in one of the apartments.

One day I walked upstairs to see my grandmother. Walking through her living room with heavy wooden furniture and rust-colored curtains, I started into the kitchen and suddenly noticed two photos side by side hanging in the hallway. I had never paid attention to them before, but I did now and a chill went up my spine. Each picture had a handsome young boy with his hair combed to the side. Each wore a red jacket with a bow tie. Unsmiling, they seemed to stare at me. I recognized their eyes from the blue faces of the soaking wet kids in my aunt's yard the day before. I knew they were dead. I did not know how they died and I was determined to find out. I needed to know. My omnipresent curiosity spurred me to look for my grandmother in another room.

I found her carefully crocheting another one of her famous afghans while watching her favorite game show. I asked who the boys were in the picture. She seemed surprised and rose from her comfortable wooden rocker to follow me to the photos. Pointing, she noted that those were her sons, my uncles. Confused and puzzled, I didn't recognize them as family and I asked why she only hung pictures of them when they were kids and I never saw them as adults.

I wanted her to tell me they had passed so I could confirm they were the two blue boys with blue skin in the driveway. Seeing them on the Other Side was normal for me, but seeing blood relatives was not and I grieved for them and for the knowing and realization that any one I knew and loved here on earth could be lost to me in this life.

I dealt with other people's kids, grandparents, aunts or friends. Having to face my own grief over death was going to be harder than I expected and the idea totally unnerved me. There was no reason to think I would be saved from that bereavement. Those I loved once were dead and those I loved now would be dead some day, too.

My grandmother walked over to a bar. From a drawer underneath, she pulled out a shoe box filled with old photos and memorabilia including yellowed newspaper clippings. One article written in French showed a photo of men dragging out bodies from a river. As we were looking at the pictures, the phone rang and my grandmother left to answer it.

Perfect timing.

I wanted to be alone with the information just given to me.

Even though I couldn't understand the French, I held onto the article with both hands and became absorbed in a vision. I felt my body submerged under water and heard the screams of the boys and on-lookers standing on a bridge. Suffocating, the musty odor of wet moss and death loomed around me as I stood in my grandmother's living room and felt a hopeless loss looking at the two boys in the bottom of the dirty river.

The boys and I exchanged a respect known only between those here who see the Other Side and those who have passed. I returned the article to its box and its place in the draw which I shut quietly so my grandmother would not know I was leaving. I did not want an emotional conversation about her sons. I did not know at that time that my grandmother also had a gift for seeing the dead. She never shared that with me. On either side.

CHAPTER 11

I went home to the comfort of the basement closet and Bobby after the episode with the boys. He was not there but something else was. A horrible red face glowed from the back cement wall clearly saying my name. Severe pain in my head warned me of evil. The red face began to slur in its own eerie language and I ran up and out into the sunlight hearing Bobby laugh and asking me if I had seen a ghost. Wiping beads of sweat off my forehead with clammy hands, I told him I had seen a ghost or demon or something.

Shaken, I ran out to the back yard to the old oak tree on which I had carved my initials weeks before. I hung upside down and Bobby decided to do the same thing. In spite of my angst, I thought it was the perfect position near his see-through face to kiss him. No one would know or see me do it because he was invisible. Part of me knew I wanted to do it. Part of me knew I could not.

I spun off the thick branch and landed on both feet and explained I had to go in for dinner and I thought it would be best for him not to come into the house. He looked puzzled and with a quick pop disappeared. He was gone. I stood alone next to the tall oak and climbed back up again. Clipping off a sharp twig to use, I carved his initials next to mine in a place on the soft bark. My behavior was that of a typical adolescent, something Bobby would never know because he was on the Other Side.

That evening, I dreamed of a house fire. I smelled the smoke as screams pierced my ears. I saw the orange color glowing into my bedroom window. Tossing in unrest, I heard the screech of sirens. I thought I was still dreaming.

I was not.

The house down the street was on fire. Dogs barked wildly and the emergency crews were fighting heavy smoke and flames. I listened to the police yelling to the crowd standing around.

Watching from my open window, I hoped every one got out of the apartment building safely. The acrid smoke started coming in the window and I closed it and the shade to escape my nightmare, a bad dream that others were literally enduring. I could still see the blood red lights throbbing from the emergency vehicles. Pulling the blankets over my head, I lay awake and waited for hours for all the different sounds to go away.

Just before drifting off to sleep, I looked out the window one last time to see a dog howling at the house in my neighbor's yard. The next day, I discovered that the dog had died in the fire. I mourned the loss of this pet and told him all would be well. He ran through the wall of the house and never returned.

CHAPTER 12

The man in black returned to me several times. He spoke nothing but I felt incredibly uncomfortable and ill when he was around in spite of the fact I thought I could control him. Wondering if Bobby had anything to do with the man in black, I dug up the nerve to ask him if there were something between him and this man. Whenever I saw the man in black, Bobby was never there, but Bobby would appear within minutes.

He quizzed me about the man's appearance.

"He wears a black suit and an old pilgrim hat. He's old and wrinkly and makes me very nervous, but I don't let it show, though." I told him.

"That's him! The gentleman I was telling you about. When did you see him?" he asked.

I answered and although it had an air of accusation, I spoke.

"I see him right before I see you. It's strange because I would see him first, then shortly after, you would come along. Weird if you ask me."

"It's not weird. But, I do have to ask why he doesn't talk to you. When I'm with him, he never shuts up. He talks about God, kids and what he'd do with all of us."

"What do you mean, what he'd do with all of us?" My apprehension grew. I knew deep down this man was up to NO good and the things Bobby was saying were proving it.

Bobby immediately countered back. "This is why I didn't tell you about him because I knew you would turn me against him somehow. He said you would do it and you are."

He popped out of sight and I tried to call him back. I needed to see the Bible. Running back into my house, I looked for the ivory colored large book that was always kept handy. The gold letters and its pages were a treasure to me, holding needed answers. Finding it, I flipped through each gilded-edged page perusing the beautiful pictures and looking for a specific drawing. My fingers raced as I desperately sought to find information on this filth Bobby was leaning toward. I found it.

Betrothed to the hells of the earth, he had horns like a goat and angry eyes in red skin. Storm clouds hurling lightening deep into the underground thrashed him where he was a lost soul now confined to the deepest realms of the holy sanctity. His screams came through the painting and angels guarded and protected the sky above with the truth of their curvy winged bodies and swords.

God's blue and white clouds of Heaven conquered this hideous fiend and I saw it emerging to me in detail. A tear ran down my face. I smoothed my hand over the worn pages and knew for sure that this face was the one I had been seeing as Bobby's gentleman all this time. No question about it. It was also the one I saw on the basement wall and the one transposed to an old man's body. It was time for me to make the choice of continuing to help people on the other side or to give it up. I was in danger and perhaps putting people I loved at risk from it.

I succumbed thinking the evil one had won the fight and maybe the war. I was afraid to go on with the battle. My trust was not strong enough to think I would be saved from this enemy by a higher being. The green fog and the boney beings were nothing compared to this man. Every part of me knew he was stronger than the skeletons. I was not sure I could win and I continued to wage my own battle of choices. If I stopped helping those on the Other Side, I might lose Bobby as well. I was totally befuddled until a few weeks later when I learned we were moving to another state. Maybe the decision had been made for me.

I was torn again, this time between relief and consternation because of Bobby.

"Could I go with you?" Bobby asked when I told him of the new house.

"I think so. You should be able to pop in and out, right?"

I was afraid of his answer.

"Well, hopefully. The old man says he'll never leave me and doesn't want me to go. I have too much work to do here."

Bobby looked away suddenly and the blue eyes that were often in my dreams were now at a far away place.

"I won't and can't leave you. I'll find a way to stay, maybe move in with a friend. Who knows, I'll figure it out. I can't leave here without you.

What would I do? Where would I go? Who would protect me from the boogey man?" I asked.

"Your spirit guides would protect you. They're around all the time. The two of them follow you like puppy dogs until you mess up or ask for something and they go running to get it for you."

Sadly, he wiped his face, trying to hide what seemed like a tear. He was still a kid in his world. I was a kid in my world. Hands in pockets, he looked around going lost in his place and clearly showing he didn't want to be around me at that time. He was trying to break free.

We said our goodbyes. The moving plans were firm and of course I had no choice but to go to a strange place. I was heartbroken to leave my familiar home like any kid would be but I had the burden of other things going on with me. The grief was insurmountable, mostly from not knowing if I'd ever see Bobby again. I felt I had just lost him to his spiritual place, a place I knew so well. I cried for days in grief and confusion and then one day I just knew that regardless of where I went, Bobby and the old man would come, too.

CHAPTER 13

Thunder boomed and lightning cracked the dark of the night sky through the window glass of my bedroom in my new home. I lay on my back and caught a glimpse of the black-brimmed hat over my head. Confused, I thought I was seeing things. I know I saw the old man next to my bed, but when the lightning left, so did he. I did not feel Bobby, but I knew he and his gentleman had followed me here because they were always together. I went back to sleep.

    This latest house was the biggest I had ever lived in. I guess the spirits figured there was lots of room. They did not go away. They talked my ear off while eating cereal at our oversized counter or joined me for a walk in the thick woods behind our home. I made quick headway in picking up the different types of energy from anyone I could not actually see. Some showed themselves; some did not. I could smell pipe tobacco or feel a leg breaking. What I was not prepared for was how smart they were and that I was in a precarious position.

    Some of my ghosts liked to play games; others only wanted to share their stories of how they died and ended up on the Other Side. Some of their antics were amusing and some distressing. I was comfortable with most of the many spirits who courted me here, but I was also a kid and not ready to hear about a woman spirit from the nineteenth century telling me how she lost her child. It depressed me, but I thought the hormone change of puberty and the homesickness for my old house were to blame. However, I did meet friends in the new place. And, they were both alive. Our summer days were spent riding our bikes or four wheelers or simply hanging out in the woods.

    For a time, it actually felt awesome combining the spirit world with the real world, like experiencing the house being built next door. The foot print was absolutely square and just a wooden frame and window cut outs were done when four of us in the neighborhood, two boys and another girl, explored the unfinished construction.

We all hung out together. We would wander the inside of the house being built trying to figure out the blueprint and choosing which bedroom we would want if we were going to live there. It was imaginary play in real life. I was over thirteen and it was time for me to experience first kisses and quick intimate touches that meant "I like you". That was as far as I would go.

We used to go to into the woods and strip down to swim. We were all in the same class and were aware of all our bodies changing. Skinny dipping made us more aware. Both boys were a love interest to me. Then when I kissed one of them, I realized my feelings were strictly platonic. He was like a brother. However, his friend was a definite chemical match.

My attraction to him distracted me from my relationship with Bobby. I knew I could not physically feel a touch or kiss from a ghost. Real fingers and lips were more appealing than those of a boy who has been dead for years. I was turning fourteen then and shifting to a more physical than spiritual life because I was becoming tired of playing invisible games and not having anyone understand what I was feeling. I was vastly alone in such a world of magic, a world of questions that could not be answered. My thoughts turned to activities with my real friends more than helping those on the Other Side.

I would ignore the spirits by looking away during the day and at night I covered my eyes with my blanket when footsteps came around my bed. I became apathetic to them and totally without guilt for it. I never saw a red flag warning me that Bobby's gentleman had gotten his wish. I was stepping away from what I was born to do and handing him the key to my life in the other world and turning over this one as a consolation prize. My downfall was his success and as an adolescent, I never saw it coming. It was not all the boyfriends or the start of a new school year that distracted me from my life's mission, but the avoidance of not complicating my life with the difficulties of the spirit world.

I convinced myself that it was better to stay out of the Other Side. I selfishly needed to concentrate on my teen life and my approaching womanhood, particularly the interest in sex--a perfectly normal thing in growing up. Nothing was going to stand in my way of an average teen life. I saw less of those on the Other Side in spite of their longing faces because

I paid less attention to them. Unfortunately, it also gave me the time to get in trouble and explore sex more than I should have. I ran wild on this earth, metaphorically and on a four wheeler. That was much more fun than helping those who had died.

My selfishness over rode my relationship with Bobby and I separated myself from the spiritual world. A whole winter season passed and as seasons changed, so did my body and my attire. I dressed provocatively for the attention and because I liked the way I looked.

No Bobby now.

No spirits now.

Nothing from the unknown was interrupting my life and I liked it.

The start of my sophomore year was as tough as my freshmen year. I had no new friends other than my immediate neighbors. During the winter, I didn't see them as much because the harsh weather kept us inside to ourselves. I was a normal teen. I had pimples. I gossiped. I tried to be sensational and wanted attention. I made $400 a week working seven days as a waitress in a local fast food place. My grades and social life went down hill fast. I went from an A student to below average.

My quest was to save money for a car and license within two years. I had no time for my friends. My full curly hair and heavy make up didn't fit with the popular group. I was an outcast because of my outfits of rocker jean jackets and my smug intuitive look at people when I knew they were lying. My psychic ability I had tried to ignore was coming back full force. I started answering questions from those who would listen and my predictions came true, even though it sometimes scared other teens. I continued to do spiritual things.

Teen girls at that time were heavy into the Oui Ja boards with a séance. It drove me nuts. Every sleep over or house party would present a circle of kids trying to not be afraid but they were even though they saw nothing and I saw everything. So, I began to take over the games. I felt powerful seeing the dead. I used the board to propel my reputation. I would be cool if things happened and they knew it. I was impressed with the fact I could talk to a spirit through the board. It was my first show off experience.

I was in the basement of a girlfriend's house. There were three of us girls in a playhouse, like a fort in her cellar. We lit candles, held hands and asked for spirits to join us and answer questions. We had a makeshift board. Minutes went by. Our skinny fingers shook. Waiting for answers, we laughed. Nothing happened. I was patient enough to wait for something to happen. Candles flickered from their wax in our circle. The flames grew taller rising high as a breeze entered the playhouse with walls made of sheets. I knew someone—a spirit—had come. One of the girls was too scared to keep her hand on the board, but two of us continued. The piece we were holding on the board became erratic as if urgently trying to communicate. It spelled out a man's name.

With reverence and respect for the dead, I wasn't sure I should continue. It was a door that would be open again. I was amazed that the spirits could go through a board and not someone like me who had the gift. The girl who lived in her house said that was her grandfather's name. She thought it was strange and of course, to me, it was the typical. The grandfather had many things to say to his son, the girl's father. He told of the emotional difficulties in the family, particularly those of the mother. According to the grandfather, they were also hoarders.

Knowing we would be in trouble because the girl's family was so religious, we cleaned up all the paraphernalia. As we left the basement, I took notes. The grandfather's ghost was adamant that what he had to say was important in order to help his family. I needed to leave it for them to read, but the place was a mess with stuff and I was afraid they would not find the paper. The dining room table seemed the spot because that was where the father unloaded his computer stuff at the end of the day. If I put the note there, he would find his father's important message from the Other Side.

I had once again helped the dead. The old warm comfortable feelings came back to me letting me know I was still capable of handling a spirit.

I would be handling a lot more sooner than later.

CHAPTER 14

Rain pounded over our big house. Sitting in the kitchen, I wanted to go outside so badly that I put on my shoes just in case the rain stopped. Thirty minutes later, still no sun shine. Taking off my shoes, I headed to my bedroom for an afternoon of basic nothingness typical of a 13-year old. Flipping through a tabloid, I could see the figure of a woman just outside my doorway. I ignored her because I was enjoying my afternoon of boredom and did not want the company of a ghost.

She just stood there in a shirt waist dress dated maybe from 1950. Her short dark hair was coiffed and her snow white face was colored by just a touch of bright lipstick. She stared at me lovingly, so I was not afraid, but I thought it was strange for her to be standing there so long without saying a word. I surreptitiously looked out of the corner of my left eye and decided she was not going anywhere, so I continued to sit on my bed. She took it as an invitation to walk in. Setting down my reading material, I waited.

Nothing.

We stared at one another mentally taking notes on the other's appearance, something women obviously do on the Other Side, too. With a smile, she folded her hands in front of her and glided back towards the door, never taking her eyes off my face. Once she entered the hallway, she was gone.

For a moment, I felt the love she had for me. It was apparent she was comfortable in the house I called home but she certainly didn't look like she belonged in the present. Heading downstairs after this encounter, I noticed the rain stopped and I wanted to enjoy a little time outdoors before it started up again. I headed out.

Passing the second flight of stairs, a picture stared at me from a wall on which hung dozens of old photos that I had just ignored in the past. No one ever talked about the photos or who was in them. It was a woman, who I knew was my paternal grandmother. She died in her early thirties when my father was two years old. I was touched by the moments she shared with me in my bedroom from the Other Side and I took it as a sign that she approved of my gift. Her silence and the peaceful look on her face showed me that I was special and blessed. Exchanging words was not necessary for me to know and understand her love as she stood so close to me. If I had not trusted and felt comfortable with her as a spirit, I could not have tolerated being with her.

Walking out of the side door of the house, I sat on the cement steps thinking of how weird my life was. Here I was a teenager who could see and communicate with ghosts. Knees up, I hugged my skinny legs and wondered how long I would be able to do this, if it would continue as I aged and if I had kids some day, would I pass it on. Then I asked myself what would be an appropriate time to tell my current boyfriend of six months that I could see spirits. The answer came easily to me.

Never.

CHAPTER 15

I knew my gift was not my choice. I could not block my intuitive sight of nightly visitors or random ghosts in the supermarket or spirits popping up at any time. Taking a deep breath, I had an overwhelming sense of duty and responsibility for what I could see and do and I was not sure I could handle it. All I wanted were the normal things of going to concerts, talking on the phone and enjoying the ordinary life of a teen, but the souls who had passed who were always waiting in line at my front cement steps would not allow me that freedom so I might as well go with it.

Now, I started sharing with everyone—friends, family, anyone who would listen. Some would be afraid and anxious. Some were not. I was flattered by those who showed an interest. That is when I became consciously aware of being sensitive to the people I was reading. I knew when to pull back. I knew when not to pull back. Those who would gossip criticized me. Those who were afraid called me a witch. My true friends thought it was the best thing ever.

I was famous.

I was infamous.

It was a dichotomy that I had to balance and live with.

Little did I realize at that time that the army of good spirits was growing to great numbers. They were cheerleaders building my confidence. They knew my pain and witnessed the emotional and verbal abuse I was getting for my gift. They were my champions. On the other hand, their assurance was being undermined by some of my peers who called me crazy and chanted to me to go to Salem, Massachusetts to get hanged. They were the ones using a Oui Ja board. They had séances and bought silly books on spells and voo doo dolls.

They were clueless and executing what would be considered black magic putting them in an environment where they had no clue what they were inviting in. They were uncontrolled and uneducated to the spiritual world. I was the object of scorn and I did dress differently with big hair and heavy makeup, but I was the real thing and dealt only in good and the more positive aspects. I never missed mass or church activities. My true friends knew I was very religious. Others just continued to ridicule.

Trying to ignore them was not working and the only way I knew how to deal with them was to benignly give it right back. I would say things to scare them like "someone's watching you" or "how did you sleep last night?" I left notes with the word "boo" in their lockers or books. I never did any significant stuff, only teasing type things. Their reactions were priceless. I had scared them out of using their black magic and I was done taking their abuse. And, by stopping them, I stopped more than peer harassment. I stopped Bobby's gentleman from doing his thing with them.

I was still so frustrated in trying to do good things for the dead and good things for my teen friends who were alive at the same time, but I was still ostracized for practicing witch craft. Parents said I was scaring their kids. However, I had reached a point where I did not care what people said about me. There was nothing wrong with me. Every one else could take a hike.

One weekend, I bought a set of Tarot cards. One hundred cards in a universal tone of stars, planets and spiritual teachings and I were alone in a room. I took a deep breath and thought of a particular person, place or thing. I never read the directions because I trusted my gut on where to place the cards. My intuition would be right. The cards fell into the right place.

I was 16 years old and started doing consistent readings for friends and their relatives. I would clandestinely hide the cards in my white leather purse keeping them safe from those who would make fun of me. I loved doing the readings. I heard answers that loved ones needed to hear. Through the magic of the cards--and it WAS magic to a 16-year-old--I could see dead loved ones and speak to them and share with the living.

The reactions were nothing but astonishment from those I read. The ten dollars wasn't bad, either. I would say thank you and wait for the next customer. I still was not doing it for the money. In actuality, I never asked for money. They just gave me whatever they wanted to give. In fact, two years before I had a tarot reader do my cards and she charged me twenty-five dollars!

During that time, my nightmares that had been so desperate, so real and so hideous were few and far between. Bobby stayed close by and watched as I would handle someone's response to something I said during a reading. He was agitated at the lack of time I had for him because I had a waitress job, relationships with friends and had to study. I was losing my best friend. I felt his energy in anger and sadness and it brought me to tears. I felt his distress and I suffered. Then, I realized I was absorbing his senses. I asked him to take his pain away from me.

Now I was really heavy into experiencing the sensory feelings--emotional and physical pain--of those on the Other Side and it hurt. I had to explain to Bobby that I could not go on feeling the discomfort of his resentment because I had to still live in the physical world. It was a concept I finally understood. I reminded myself to tell every spirit to hold any sensory feelings so I could be more available to help them. They had to comply or I would not be able to help them. I had to take care of myself. There were so many of them and only one of me. I was comfortable helping those in both worlds and I took more control of the messages. Once again, I was a spiritual person and asked for protection from the white light of the beings shown to me and from the Lord's Prayer.

Now, I had to figure out how to make Bobby feel better.

And, to pass my driver's ed exam.

CHAPTER 16

After two tries and side swiping the bumper on another vehicle trying to parallel park, I passed my driver's test. Two weeks later, I received the coveted plastic card. With a huge smile on my face and a year left in high school, I knew I had to forge ahead in spite of the ridicule and judgment and continue to work hard on my grades and job. Both spiritual and physical worlds kept me busy and preoccupied enough so I was not distracted by all the daily energies constantly surrounding me.

I took the time to open my spiritual door and kept up with the Tarot cards and readings. Bobby was still at my side along with two other figures garbed in robes. One of the ghosts was a blonde blue-eyed handsome six feet of man who looked like a California surfer. The other was short, around my height of five feet. His dark hair was thinning from the front. He had thick fingers and big hands and spoke with a Jersey Shore dialect. Both men would argue right in front of me about what choices would be the right ones for me to make. Ironically, they came out equal in their decisions, but whatever decisions I made would be mine alone. I had the free will. They gave me the final decision. Later, I would call them my spirit guides.

My guides would help during the readings by answering my questions or just by being there for spiritual support. I paid attention to every word they said. They protected me like bouncers in a bar and would genuinely love me for who I was. Whenever I would help a human or a spirit in any capacity, my guides were there to walk me through it all and my trust with them grew stronger.

I knew they were sent to me for me and it was not long before I comprehended the fact that everyone had guides and the only way they are able to help us is when we ask them. On alert and ready, they wait to hear the words from those who need and they satisfy only if it is for the highest good. Lessons are to be learned in the process and all in good faith. I understood it had to be and I knew many people felt a voice within they called their intuition or their gut instinct. I called it spirit guides and defined it not as protective angels, but rather guides who help out in the journey of life. They were chosen because they have the knowledge and unconditional love to be there for anyone regardless of race, color or religion. The connection to a spirit guide can be very strong and if utilized properly, people would make fewer and fewer mistakes by just listening to the inner voice of a higher source.

As a teen, the most difficult part in my knowing of guides, premonitions, past spirits and so on was when I had a foreshadowing about an acquaintance or friend being in an automobile accident. I knew when someone would become pregnant. I would know before anyone else on earth knew things. Most teens would not want the burden of knowing what was going to happen, but I had to handle that foreshadowing along with the onus of school and keeping up my grades to graduate.

Instead of taking a full curriculum at college right out of high school, I chose to work full time and take a few education courses. My energy was insurmountable because I used my daily prayers and meditation to keep my mind clear from distractions of stress or romantic involvements. My conscious and subconscious mind could hold vast amounts of information intuitively and collectively. Because I felt invulnerable, invincible and attractive, I lead a magical but dangerous life. My protective spirit guides and a higher power were with me and I gladly accepted it. In my reasoning, I could live as I wanted, no matter what I did because they had my back.

Little did I know, that was not the truth.

CHAPTER 17

My twenties began in a fury and with total disregard for the feelings of others. I did not notice any of the warnings put to me by the universe. Being twenty-one gave me the right to drink, drink and drink some more with friends, family or simply alone. I remember even drinking on the job and savoring every last drop of a shot that was mistakenly left on the bar where I worked. Being careful was not an operative phrase to me. My behavioral patterns combined with alcohol altered my spiritual life. I was less in control of my thoughts or who I was. I could not think on my own.

The gentleman was playing a huge part in this because my downward spiral into temptations kept me away from what I really enjoyed--helping others. I was in no shape to do that or even help myself. I toppled more into an abyss of decadence aided by my size six tight clothes, large breasts, high heels and loud music. I dropped college classes and paid as much attention to men as I did alcohol. For years I was obsessed with sex, men and booze—entanglements that lasted for months into years. I was lost, dishonest and unforgiving, blaming others for their misadventures, but never taking responsibility for my own actions and repercussions.

I was the ripe old age of 23 when the truth dawned on me--the gentleman was winning again. He had taken control of my life as well as taken away the confidence and love that I spiritually experienced. Actually, I should say I freely gave up all that goodness that was mine, but my intuitiveness never strayed for others who needed help. I was blind to helping myself with alcohol, drugs and sex. I knew my spirit guides were not far away, but I could not see them clearly. My sensory was not totally closed off, but my ego overpowered my ability to ask for help and it was easy to blame others for my vile actions than to take the responsibility for my behavior. I figured my guides had abandoned me.

Knowing my guides would not approve of my current life choices, I decided not to ask them for anything for the time being. I still had psychic ability and the ghosts who hung around me were now the ones who could relate to my current life style. They had once lived the party life I was now living. They belonged to the gentlemen who had worked his way into my life destroying everything in his path like a tornado. I was not strong enough to ask for help. I continued my recklessness, a life of nothingness that was everything to me at the same time.

Then, I had a vision.

CHAPTER 18

His height was just under six feet. With broad shoulders, olive skin, dark hair and a gorgeous smile that that would melt any woman's heart, he had the arms and hands of a gladiator and the voice of a poet. His strong hands held mine. Wisps of hair flew in my face as I laughed and his laugh echoed mine with a mutual need. Naked, we made love and sexually explored each other. Holding one another, we floated down to the ground to a field of long soft grass, our bodies moving together. Just before we climaxed, I glanced in the direction of a tree and saw Bobby and his gentlemen. Standing in a panic, I realized there was no dark haired gladiator to protect me, absolutely no hint of his presence anywhere. I felt a hopeless loss at his absence and at the disappointment on Bobby's face.

Hoping to regain some dignity, I ran to Bobby. His face showed no forgiveness. I wept at his feet and the feet of the gentleman. Blinding me, blood dripped from my eyes. I gave up trying to wipe it away and falling to the hard ground, I accepted my failure assuming I had failed another test, even in my dreams. I had succumbed again to only my pleasure not thinking of the feelings of anyone else. The meaning of love was lost to me. As thunder boomed, rain assaulted my naked body and rinsed the blood stains off me.

I screamed, "Why are you doing this to me? Why?"

The powerful heat from the sun dried me off with forgiveness.

I awoke to despondency in a lonely apartment with two cats and a wish that I could escape from the same mistakes I was making in my real life. I wanted some one, some thing, to take me away to a place where there would be no madness like that I was living on earth. Then, realization struck again that deep in sleep, my subconscious mind would be more receptive to spiritual visitors with whom I could enjoy a dream or two in the convenience of my bed. They had come to me in visions of beaches, kites or simply eating food.

The nightmares were another thing entirely. I was not safe in my sleep and evil came to inflict pain and scar me when I was vulnerable. Awake, my conscious mind helped me rationalize dreams and keep me sane. Nightly visitors came when I was awake, too, but they would know that the blankets over my head meant I needed privacy. My mind was closed to them.

Not everything was always closed, though. Friends would visit my apartment and hear a knock here, a voice there or a door or window slamming shut right in front of them for no reason. They knew of my gift and were surprised to realize that no matter where I lived, the haunting would live there. I knew the ghosts did not possess the residence.

They possessed me.

It was not a haunted place to me because I knew why and I knew who the pesky guests were who were at work scraping the walls or whispering my name as I watched a movie or was in bed with my boyfriend. I knew who pulled the blankets off us when we were in bed and why the toilet would flush or the bedroom door would open slowly when no one else was in the house.

I would say simply, "Welcome to my life."

Jokes, laughter and a few beers calmed the nerves of my guests and neighbors.

Most of the time.

But not all of the time.

CHAPTER 19

One day, I was bringing out the trash and overheard a male neighbor's conversation to another man about his apartment being haunted. Taking my time with the garbage, I listened to what he was saying word for word about his ghostly visitor. The two men were leaning on a wall. The one being haunted described his ghost.

"He was wearing a black top hat and dark suit. Probably around 70 years old and he talks to my daughter every night."

Seeing me approach, he sheepishly stopped talking and averted his face, but I had heard just enough of the description to make me drop my house keys. I did not know either man, but I walked right up to them and apologized for intruding.

"Did you say your apartment is haunted?" I bluntly asked.

Checking me out, he straightened out his shirt and admitted he thought it was true.

With an attempt to make him comfortable, I told him I had seen the gentleman several times and that he should not be concerned about the old man, but the welfare of his child who lived there should be considered because children are more vulnerable to spiritual entities.

He acquiesced to my request at taking a walk through his apartment. When we went in, I saw it was in desperate need of a good cleaning, physically and maybe spirit-wise. We walked through each room and my intuition sent off alarms of something or someone nearby. I asked permission to walk into his daughter's room and I opened the closet door. A jewelry box began to play as a ballerina softly danced around. My neighbor started to shake. White faced, he told me it was impossible for the box to work because he had removed the motor, spring and bolts from it a few months back because his daughter would wake up in the middle of the night with the box playing eerie music—the box with no motor that was now playing in my hands.

After sharing stories that seemed to help mollify him, he seemed to be less frightened. Back in my apartment, I took aspirin for my headache and fell asleep. I was awakened by a screech from hell that seemed like it came from right outside my bedroom door. I sat up in bed and watched my bedroom door open very slowly. The face of my nemesis, the gentleman, was reflected in the mirror next to the door, his smug smile directing my attention to the bathroom. Tentatively walking in the direction of splashing water, I saw a young man dressed in clothing indigenous to 1970.

The pungent smell of alcohol and pot permeated the room. A blood curdling scream came out a young woman in the bathtub as she started to gasp for air. He was holding her long brown hair plunging her head under the water in the claw foot tub. Holding her head down, he looked at me.

Hard rock belted from a music source as I rushed in to stop him from drowning her. I could not breathe. Holding the front of my neck, I tried to get air and could not. Panicking, I held onto the sink and focused at the mirror where the gentleman was standing. Somehow I knew I would die if the young woman drowned under that water.

Falling to the floor, I pounded the blue carpet with my fist crying for help and the forgiveness of all my sins. Vomiting, I suddenly noticed the music stopped blaring. The two people who had invaded my bathroom were gone. The gentleman quietly left. Standing, I looked in the mirror. My usual summer tan was bluish white. Every inch of my body was wracked in pain. I crawled into bed wanting my life to be over to escape such violence.

The next day and with great deliberation, I headed to a spiritual store where I gathered holy water, rosaries, Catholic ornaments and religious pictures with which to wall paper the apartment. I figured after the night from hell, I should do what I could to protect myself from things like that happening again. I came across a bucket filled with bundles of dried green leaves and I read the inscription on its embossed ticket.

"Sage is a form of plant that may be used for the cleansing or ridding of any negative energy in one's environment."

That was just what I was looking for.

Dropping the money on the counter, I literally ran out of the store not even asking if I needed instructions on how to use it. I gauged what might be appropriate and spread the herb inside and out of the apartment along with all my new spiritual icons. This anointment gave me blessings for about one month until one night when I came home from a late shift at the restaurant.

Impatient and exhausted, I could not deal with the typical all night party going on with the people in the apartment above me. After knocking on their door, I found myself facing a neighbor who asked me what MY problem was because I was bugging him after eleven o'clock at night. I looked around his apartment and it was quite evident that there was not even one party-goer. I apologized and walked back to my place.

At 3:00 a.m., I awoke to the smell of cigarette smoke, loud music, tires screeching, revelry and bawdiness in general. Looking out the window, I saw nothing but a quiet autumn night with leaves blowing in the air and light traffic as usual. After climbing back into bed, I lay on my back and closed my eyes. I felt something climbing up my legs. I knew it was not one of the cats because I had shut them into a spare room so they would not wake me.

My body and mind tight as a drum, I felt the bedding smothering me. I could not scream. Pain burned my skin as blankets crushed down taking every inch of air I had. I closed my eyes not wanting to see what was doing this and hoping it would just go away. I envisioned Jesus on the cross sacrificing himself and, for a split second, thought that maybe that was what I was supposed to do. Somehow, I managed to hide my fear.

The crushing feeling ebbed slowly and I could breathe again. I didn't move for what seemed like the rest of early morning. Exhausted, I was afraid a pattern was beginning to develop at the apartment I was staying in. I decided to move out. I had seven months left on my lease, but I packed the next day, not caring what legal ramifications I would have. I knew that if I stayed there, I would die.

Being so incredibly naïve, I did not consider that the gentlemen and his army of spirits would follow.

CHAPTER 20

Tall, dark and handsome, he stood there in the middle of the diner. His muscles bulged under a tight black t-shirt and dark blue jeans. With his darkest brown eyes and black hair around an olive complexion, he was startling to me because he looked just like my Gladiator Man. I had dreamed of this man a year before. We sensed an immediate attraction and I knew he recognized me, too.

After a few minutes of banal amenities, we chatted, becoming more comfortable with one another. It turned out we lived in the same neighborhood when we were young, the area where I met Bobby and the gentlemen for the first time. The irony of seeing a man in a dream vision, a man who lived two blocks from me when I was growing up, was a bit disconcerting, but our relationship ended up in bed. It was an easy thing for me to fall into because I remembered our relationship so vividly in my dream.

Suspicious, I started wondering that if the gentlemen interrupted that beautiful dream, maybe the Gladiator Man was part of the gentlemen's entourage. I became skeptical of our relationship and the thought of my new lover being on the wrong side of good and evil making him either good or bad for me. I lay awake through endless nights waiting for the morning sun to rise and the chance to sneak away from him out a back door because of my uncertainty.

Bobby was jealous of him. When I felt his discomfort, my vision was that of me crying blood for him. It was my vision for me, not a friend or stranger, and it affected me so much that I was not about to let go if I did not have to give up the relationship. My dream had been so realistic, so intimate, that there must be a reason I could consciously touch him now in this lifetime.

We were together for several years without either of us really wanting a major commitment. We both saw other people and had lovers during this time which made it more difficult for me to think he was the chosen one for me. Late nights talking after love making were becoming fewer and few as the honesty between us challenged our relationship. Something in the line of energy or feeling was lacking from him, so I started looking elsewhere.

I still dreamed about him and would wake up crying that this man could not be a part of my life for some reason, but why on earth would he have come to me in such a loving dream and a year later come to me in reality only to be ripped away in deceit, selfishness and nearly my death.

I began to see other men regularly, that was still our mutual understanding. I loved him half the time and I was okay with that for the time being until a visit to a local beach where a girlfriend and I were flirting with college guys who prettied up the landscape playing football. One muscular six-footer caught my eye and he deliberately threw the football to land at my feet. Laughing, I told him his throw was lousy. We went out that night and it was like I had known him forever. It was lust at first sight.

About a month into our relationship, he told me he had to move out of his family home as soon as possible. His parents would no longer tolerate nor subsidize his bad behavior. It seemed simple to me to ask him to move in with me and within two weeks we found a small two bedroom place. With my money and my credit, there was no problem beginning a new life.

I always knew when I could tell a person about my gift and when I should keep it to myself, regardless of how intimate the relationship. Telling him was not an option. He never knew or suspected because I had learned to be good at hiding it.

He dropped out of school and I helped him buy a used truck. I was still managing my 50 hour a week job while discreetly managing my Gladiator Man on the side. Although Gladiator Man and I had an open relationship, I felt it would not bode well if he knew about my new interest so I kept it under wraps. It all went well for about four weeks.

The ex-college guy and I acquired a variety of pets to the point that our place looked like a pet store, but the menagerie made us feel like a family and we really enjoyed our life style. I often bragged how well my college guy treated me when I was with other friends.

The bliss lasted only a few more weeks until I noticed a dramatic change in him. He became distant, hurtful and reclusive and I was trying to figure out if he drank or took drugs or just his true self was coming out. I would wake up with him standing on the side of my bed rambling on in a nefarious rumbling and all too familiar tone. In denial, I chalked it up to him sleep walking or the oppressive heat of summer. We had no air conditioning. Eventually, I could talk him back into bed to finish a night's sleep.

Then, one night I awoke to the noise of the shower running in the bathroom down the hall. I got up and found him staring into nothing. He was standing in front of the mirror that was obscured with the steam swirling through the bathroom. I spoke his name. He did not answer. I stood next to him and felt instant intense fear. He turned and looking into my eyes, began to draw on the foggy glass.

The face of a negative entity appeared and I stepped out of the small room very slowly as if not wanting to disrupt his concentration and artwork. I closed the door to the bedroom and locked it silently hoping he would not awaken from this particular sleep walking incident. Clutching our large dog, I also hoped he would not come back into the bedroom.

After a few minutes, the dog started to growl and I saw the shadow of his feet by the door. His voice was now audible and he asked me to open the door. Recognizing his voice, the dog wagged her tail. I swung the door opened and hugged him and acted like nothing happened. After he went to sleep, I went to the bathroom to view the drawing he made and sure enough, I found what I knew was there. The face I had seen years before on the basement wall was staring straight at me. I knew then that evil had not left me.

I wiped it with my fingers and damned it to hell where it belonged. Afterwards, I climbed into the double bed, too small for my two hundred pound boy friend, the dog and me. I could have cared less. I crowded next to him and the dog and I stayed close to his warm body all night. I cried myself to sleep thinking how safe I would have been if I were with the Gladiator Man.

CHAPTER 21

Coming home from a late night shift, I noticed the apartment door was unlocked. I peered though the opening to see my boyfriend sitting on the floor in front of the television staring at a blank snowy screen like when the cable goes out. He never seemingly noticed or acknowledged me as I placed my keys on the small glass table and walked to the bathroom.

With an uneasy feeling in the pit of my stomach, I washed my hands and grabbed the hand towel still carrying it out of the bathroom. I nonchalantly asked what he was watching. Glaring at me from where he sat on the living room floor, he slowly stood. Ominously taking five steps toward me in the kitchen, he slammed his huge fist into the center of my face in one easy powerful blow and then, jumping back from me a bit, he yelled and did it again.

I ran around the table to avoid him making it into the bedroom and locked the door. The dog was with me and howling as the mad man tried to break it down. I was screaming "stop" and uselessly leaning heavily against the door that broke through easily. I screamed. The dog did nothing to protect me.

I had landed halfway on the bed. He jumped on my small frame and used his knees to pin down my arms. I tried to punch him. It was futile. He ripped my uniform shirt and grabbed my breasts roughly while biting my flesh. He covered my mouth with his big hand and used a strange voice I had never heard from him before. I looked at his face and begged for my life as he tried to strangle me.

He punched me squarely on the left side of my jaw making blood splatter on the wall and I heard my bones crack. He held my face to his and reminded me he was the one, not me. He was the one for those to listen to and he was the one to bring me to the depths of his hell. He told me he would see me there and not to underestimate his power.

His hand clung on to my face that screamed in pain. After breaking and tearing off my necklace, he ripped the rings from my fingers all the while sitting on top of me. He pulled my head back with a handful of hair and made me say he was the boss. I was crying and begging my friend inside this monster to come back to me because I knew it was something else that had taken over his body. It was a stronger and more fiendish source. And, it was using my boyfriend's huge frame to beat me physically and mentally.

He released me.

Then there was silence.

I opened my swollen eyes, nearly shut from the assault. The boyfriend had gone to the kitchen and now came back to me, clearly scared. He hugged me close and cried on my lap. My aching body began to rock back and forth as he held me in his arms apologizing for what happened. He broke his hold on me when he noticed the smashed door and the blood stains on the wall. I covered myself with the blankets from the bed holding them over my naked upper torso inflamed with his human bites. He left. I watched to make sure his truck drove off.

I took the dog and dropped her off with a friend and I went to the safest place I knew. The Gladiator Man was not home but his good friends were there. With the kitchen light off, I walked into the bedroom and woke one of them with a light shake. I needed his help. He took one look at my bloodied mutilated face and jumped out of bed. Carefully removing what was left of my shirt, he gave me one of his to wear.

I started to vomit and he held my hair back. That night was the most terrifying of my life and I slept in a water bed that was not mine with a friend who had no problem holding me while my Gladiator Man was out. I lay there with a broken jaw, several fractured bones and a future of thirteen years of nine surgeries, multiple infections and medical complications.

My college boy had truly been possessed by evil. I believed this.

All because I had tried to help those on the Other Side and help those on this side who needed answers from the Other Side.

PART THREE
SOMETHING BETTER

Better is the end of a thing than the beginning thereof.

The Bible: Ecclesiastes

CHAPTER 22

The gorgeous garden-style apartment was approximately 1200 square feet and more than enough room for me and the cats and a live-in boyfriend. I had been seeing a new man in my life for six months and the relationship developed quickly so we were living together. The Gladiator man and I decided to amicably part ways because I wanted marriage and children and he did not. With my biological clock ticking, I left him and never looked back.

My new boyfriend became my fiancé and one day while we worked in the kitchen, I confessed to him that I could communicate with the dead. Because he was witnessing so many paranormal events, I really did not have much of choice. Strange things went on in our house. Hoping he was going to take it well, I told him everything. After a bit of fidgeting, he actually seemed only slightly shocked and simply asked, "Why didn't you tell me this a year ago?"

"Look," I explained. "When I think someone will handle this news well and I tell them, they react negatively and start judging and criticizing me. I just figured you would do the same and leave me."

I was stacking dishes and put them away, a rather mundane daily chore to do in the middle of my earth-shattering news, I thought. He remained silent, gathering cardboard boxes for recycling and never said another thing. We did not bring it up again. He, I and the pets pretty much lived in harmony.

Ghostly activity in the new apartment was apparently much safer than where I had previously stayed and I realized I now had a pretty good outlook with a spring in my step, a good job and lots of friends. I continued to see Bobby who had gone back to the form of a young boy rather than physically mature with me. Therefore, I was more like his mother now and

I actually had to chastise him for being in the bedroom with my fiancé and me and discipline him more in an adult to child relationship. I saw less of the gentleman.

It took that last horrific experience for me along with prayer and meditation to come to the conclusion that my spiritual ablutions would help me forget the abuse. When I had a weak moment and dwelled on the beating I had taken, harmful things would happen and they could grow stronger and build a more solid base on which I could continue self-abuse or that to others. I had to take what I learned—what I knew—and put it to good use always remembering not to give in if an evil entity approached me again. I also knew I had to be aware of foreshadowing in the form of a migraine, nausea or bad taste in my mouth and pay attention to any warning signs that might portend danger or harm.

Those were obvious manifestations proving the enemy was around. When and if I could differentiate good from bad, I knew I would have an easier physical life. Along with the sage and prayers, I often used a white protective bubble along with what I had learned from Bobby, the spirit guides and angels. All these elements were my team against evil. As the final resolution, the Other Side was beginning to make sense to me. I knew instinctively that whenever the bad stuff happened, I was also being saved in the end and I rejoiced in that knowledge.

I would often keep a log of my dreams and take notes of whatever psychic visions or thoughts came across. Then I would reflect and check them off if they happened. I realized there were more that came true than not and I would confidently close my diary of predictions and continue to use what I learned from the others. The gentleman seemed less formidable now because I was becoming wise to him. I could function on a daily basis with the security that I knew how to keep myself safe.

We started planning our wedding six months away from the actual date of the ceremony. I really was unsure about marriage and argued with him a lot. My concern about tying the knot kept me out late at night regardless of where I went to avoid coming home. Three months before the wedding, I canceled it. The whole thing became a big nasty disaster with all the semantics of the event with the wedding dress, all deposits lost, cost of invitations out the window and the plethora of plans that come with a wedding. I totally disregarded the whole mess. Any inconvenience to me or to anyone else was worth my decision. I was not going to make a big mistake.

About that time, my grandfather passed away after a long battle with Alzheimer's. He was my first physical family member I knew as a live person and then as a spirit. Ultimately, his death was the catalyst of my reconciliation with my fiancé. One day, my grandfather pointed out stones near a grave. He said that someday these rocks would turn to dust just like the body beneath the grave and that some day I would be dust. He wanted me to get on with my life and not waste it with indecision. So, I became engaged again to the same man for a second time and we married.

We wanted a baby and I unsuccessfully tried to get pregnant for a year. Ready to give up, I was so discouraged one day that I went into our spare room and knelt on the plush tan carpet. I asked God why he had not blessed me with a child. I gave a confession of sins, I prayed the Lord's Prayer and I said Hail Mary's. Genuflecting, I fell asleep in the spare bed and soaked the pillow crying myself to sleep.

A light sleeper, I heard footsteps making their way down the wooden floor of the hallway. Thinking it was my husband returning to bed after using the bathroom, I rolled over with my arm dangling to the tan carpet. I felt a hand touching my arm and opened my eyes to a woman with brown hair in a 1950s style. Wearing bright red lipstick and dressed in off white robes, she stared at me and lifted her hand. On the tips of her fingers was a ball of light so blinding that I had to close my eyes. She nudged the orb off of her fingers and it filled the room with a glimmering essence that gave a sense of calm. Then, she and the light were gone. Five days later, I knew I was pregnant. A pharmacy early home pregnancy test confirmed this miracle.

After a very difficult pregnancy, I gave birth to a beautiful girl and we chose a name for her that means by the sea or by the ocean. Her name was significant to me because many of my past summers had been spent staying near the ocean. I loved the moods of the sea. She had her moods, too, and was not a particularly easy baby, but she was so very much wanted and loved. Everyone adored her. When the baby was a month old I learned the spirit of the woman who had visited me was a deceased relative. She had died young so I never knew her. My daughter truly was a gift from God.

CHAPTER 23

Spring came and with it, Easter. I went out to the local variety store to pick up a few things I needed. When I walked into the shop carrying my baby girl, Gladiator Man was standing there. He was not a vision. He was a real person. We were both stunned. We exchanged small talk and I noticed he wore no wedding band. He saw my diamond and condescendingly commented that HE would have bought me a bigger one, but he said the baby was beautiful.

Uncomfortable, I wrote a check for the purchases and ran out to the car where I climbed in fast and locked the doors. I was shocked at seeing him and my mind raced with thoughts that I possibly could keep running into him. Evidently, I had not moved far enough away from him physically or from the memories of him. I had to put the chance meeting behind me.

Six months later I became pregnant again. I found out on the day of our daughter's first birthday that our second child would be born in the spring. We had a light-haired son. His name meant follower of God and our daughter was nearly two when he was born. She loved him as much as she loved our cat, but we had to put down that pet when the new baby was a month old.

Filled with grief and with babies in tow, I went off to have her euthanized. Arriving home from the vet, I walked into an empty kitchen and saw the cat's bowl. Still grieving and angry with myself for not taking care of pet paraphernalia, I felt my eyes fill with tears as I put away her dish and started cutting up a banana.

"Mama, kitty is on the couch. Look!!"

I spun around, furious and confused until I realized my two-year-old WAS really looking at the spirit of our cat hanging out on a favorite place on the sofa. My suspicions were confirmed about passing on my gift. I felt our son had the gift, too because of his behavior at times.

As young as they were, it was time to teach my kids what I knew about the Other Side. Their powers were growing stronger every day and I did not want them to feel the shame or the embarrassment that I felt growing up. They would learn to help those who passed without the impediments of fear and condemnation. I would walk them through it.

At that time, my grand-father was trying to communicate with me again. I could smell his spicy cologne as well as his pungent cigarette smoke. He spoke nothing and my subconscious was not getting the message from him. I felt blocked, but then I realized it was not me, it was he. I saw the way he swayed from one end of the hallway to the other in the frustration of trying to talk to me. He spoke French when he was alive, but that was not the issue. He just could not speak at all. It was as though he had been denied the ability to talk. Then I learned why.

My guides were consciously making me aware that he had a lot of atoning to do and a lot to learn. They went on to teach me that contingent on how we live our lives, coming back to earth as a spirit to be in the presence of a physical person is a gift that must be earned unless one has been pure on this earth. Even a murderer can atone. If his actions root in evil, there will most likely not be any judgment of the higher power but that person will head in a straight direction into the dark sources.

If atonement is done before one dies, then the fruitful existence of eternal life is ready for them when they arrive on the other side. They do not have to do a formal confession. At the end of the day, any action deemed inappropriate by an individual should be accounted for on this earth by awareness of that individual. Acknowledging indiscretions is enough for atonement.

"It's earned." California Surfer Dude said with a quick wink to me.

Until he was absolved from whatever indiscretions, my grand-father had very limited time with me at each visit, but we made the most of it.

As days went on, I would see him more frequently but still for short bursts of time. Now I was beginning to hear his voice speaking in French. With my daughter on my lap, he would mistakenly call her my name and I tried to tell him that she was not me. I was me and she was my daughter. My handsome grand-parent just did not comprehend. Asking my Guides again why he looked at my daughter thinking he was looking at me, I learned that because of his dementia, his progress would be slower in learning on the Other Side. He was still in a forgetful state of mind and did not even know at times he had passed.

After knowing this, I would sit in my Canadian rocker and be unsure about what the Other Side meant exactly to different people. I was kind of pissed. Church teaches that when we die we go to this celestial peaches-and-cream place. I questioned the idea why God would let our health issues go with us when we died. A better deal should be that our impediments and maladies leave us and we move to a brighter, lighter, stress free environment. That is what I always heard in church masses or from the lips of my elders. And, I thought that was so unfair to people and spirits who were not aware that they might still hurt in their idea of Heaven. Man has perpetuated the myths and added ideas for what man believes.

Totally not fair.

I started taking notes about every spirit I could remember and how they passed, their mental and physical functions or lack thereof in the magical place of Heaven. When I narrowed the pros and cons, I figured out that we are responsible and we are 100% involved in every choice of our lives. We have to maintain a certain level of living in order to receive the wonderful gifts of the higher source when we pass. The higher source helps with what we need to learn and provides the resources of angels and guides in our physical lifetime. The guides are there in our spiritual lifetime, too. We are never alone.

All of this added to what I had to do with the spirits on the Other Side and people who would become spirits when they passed from earth. There had to be an easier way for harmony to exist. I started to share this secret with everyone. If I knew someone in a hospice situation, I would try to visit them. I made suggestions for atonement so they could have a choice and perhaps not be surprised and suffer after they died. They could automatically enjoy the amenities offered on the Other Side.

I was trying to benefit the living, the dying and the dead.

The benefits of forgiveness and taking responsibility were major factors and, of course, a belief in any higher being helped immensely. I learned there is no need to search for forgiveness or ask for it face to face with the person from whom you need forgiveness. Feeling the forgiveness within us is what helps. All you do in life and the way you die are a huge part of acceptance and healing on the Other Side. In addition, the quicker people come to terms with passing, the better and quicker that healing begins.

Spirits due not recognize immediately that they are dead and those who pass grieve as hard as those left behind.

As far as my grandfather was concerned, he began to earn his time and his memory and eventually, he could smile and pat me on the head, knowing the difference between my daughter and me.

CHAPTER 24

With two children now, we had outgrown our house, and my life was still so full and busy that it was easier for me to leave Gladiator Man and my insane past behind. Within five days of putting our property on the market, we sold it for double what it was worth. After buying land in another town and in more of an urban area, we built another home.

Life was moving way too fast for me and with the kids and a cat to care for along with the many spirits who came along, I was feeling emotionally and physically drained, but I kept in touch with my spiritual roots and showed my children how to pray and ask for the white light for protection. They looked at pictures of angels and I would explain who each one was and what their jobs were.

Our daughter seemed to appreciate all I was teaching her, all she was learning. I would discover her with her bedroom door ajar talking to herself or someone else. I let her do what she was born to do, only intervening when I thought it necessary. She was three. Our son was just one and showed his high sensory capacity only when he was in crowds of people. He would just cry and cry, obviously consumed by so many energies at the same time. His little mind could not understand it all. Every day, he would cry for what seemed like hours at a time, reminding me of when I was his age and had to seek refuge with the television in my room.

Seeing him go through this, I became depressed. After much soul searching, I sought help from a psychiatrist. After two weeks, I figured out I was not the wacky one. The highly recommended doctor was batty. After pushing me into the antidepressant drugs direction, I encouraged HIM to see someone. Leaving his office, I realized I needed a more spiritual and subtle approach. I needed someone who could understand who and what

I was—more than just a mother of two who had inherited their mother's psychic abilities.

And, one day, there she was in the form of a new therapist. With gray hair bobbed to her neck and silver rimmed glasses, she handed me pages and pages to sign on the dotted line contracting me for six weeks of sessions that would cost an absolutely obscene amount of money. Desperately seeking peace in my life regardless of the cost, I signed on that dotted line.

We began with meditations and she would record each session taking notes while we sat for an hour and a half each week. As she listened to the tape recordings again and again, she noticed audible voices in the background of our conversations. She knew this was weird because we were always alone in the office and we were never interrupted. She was astounded that week after week, voices other than hers and mine would end up on the tape recording. We both decided that the verbalization was that of spirits. Assuming there was something that the spirit world needed to tell me, she decided to change my therapy. She put me under hypnosis by ringing a few bells while I listened to soothing music. I fell fast and easy.

I went into a scene on a beach when I was twelve wearing a sleeveless white shirt and blue shorts. I walked into the waves feeling the salty water on my body without fear of drowning as I went totally under the spell and under the ocean. When I started to convulse, she told me that I was safe and asked me to come out of the water. I did. Then I was in the present and was walking to a nearby cliff that I had to climb. The mountain was treacherous, spiked with pointed rocks and prowled by wild animals. Feet bloodied and clothing dirtied, I made it to the top sobbing my heart out.

Looking out over the cliff, I saw a very large hawk flying toward me. With one swift swoosh, he grabbed me taking me up across the ocean higher and higher to what seemed like paradise where he dropped me on a marble floor. I was no longer dirty and wore a shiny robe just like the others who stood around me. They floated, not walked. I went up stairs to a massive marble building supported by huge columns. I noticed those around me were still dressed in the robes and they whispered as I walked by.

I saw two beings I had recognized from years before as my spirit guides. They stood around a circular table. I greeted them quietly because I was afraid to speak up. They gave me a look of acceptance. With a gentle touch on my shoulder, my spirit guide who looked like the California surfer pointed to a book that was way bigger than any book I had ever seen or imagined. He opened it to reveal a piece of parchment under which I could see my birth certificate.

He showed me my entire life in what seemed like minutes—the good and the bad—and he pointed out how my guides had stood by me throughout my life. Bobby was also a factor in the memories and I laughed and cried at seeing him. Those moments when I had felt so weak, so alone, I was always loved and cared for. As each page turned, I knew the end was imminent. I was told I could ask a question. Subconscious to subconscious, no lips physically moving, I asked them to tell me my purpose for this life.

They brought me to a red carpet that had a huge gold chair encrusted with jewels and covered with food. I began to feel a breeze as I sat on the chair and I felt like a queen looking down at all over her servants. I relished in that glory for only a minute before the crowd dispersed making way for someone to walk up the red carpeted path. In awe and in fright, I saw Jesus, the Savior known to me and the air was filled with an almost elusive pure smell reminding me of clean mist or that soft powdery fragrance from only newborn baby.

Mother Mary was behind Jesus. Tears filled my eyes. Instinct told me to get out of the royal chair because I did not deserve it. I fell on my knees seeing His Holy Feet before me. I kissed them. My head bowed, he placed his hands on my chin lifting it so I could see his face. He spoke to me and reminded me I was his child and I deserve to be one of Glory, for I was a child of God. The words of sanctity say I was chosen as the One and should be so. I would be rewarded with my efforts as long as I shared my gifts with love. He turned and walked away and I followed Him, not wanting to leave His side.

"No!" he said, gesturing with His hand that I should turn around. He told me it wasn't my time and I had to go back. He reminded me to remember what He said, because I had a few more mountains to climb before I reached His Glory. As He walked out of the room that overflowed with food and water, I realized that I already had my rewards and I should stop looking, but I also knew that I had to continue using my gift because it was making a difference in this world.

CHAPTER 25

After that vision, I was feeling much better about things, but life soon brought more trials and travails taking care of the two babies and dealing with the severe health issues of my husband. Surgeries forced him to be out of work for long periods of time and then he lost his job. Thousands and thousands of dollars in medical bills piled up. Financial distress depleted our assets just about the time that the economy was weak.

It was difficult to pretend things were fine to everyone. We were so worried about the lack of money, but worse, during all this, my husband was diagnosed with a very rare form of cancer on the bones under his arm. We were devastated and petrified. After two months of tests, biopsies and whatever the doctors were doing, they finally scheduled surgery, an operation that would determine our future.

The night before we had to head to the hospital, I was tucking in our little daughter who announced, "The angels said Daddy would be fine."

I sat on the bed not knowing if I should believe her or not. I asked her what angels and she continued to tell me how she had seen five angels and a unicorn enter her room. They had danced in a circle with shimmering glitter all around and one whispered to her that Daddy would be fine. She noted how they disappeared shortly after and she wished they had stayed.

I thanked her for sharing the message and left the room sobbing with emotion and stress. I went into my office to check e-mails before I headed for bed myself. Lowering myself into my over-sized desk chair, I looked at my screen saver constantly changing scenes. An image immediately caught my eye. Dressed in white, five angels, replete with halos, were standing in a circle. Glitter was everywhere in the purple background.

There was no unicorn in this scene, but I knew immediately a higher source had sent confirmation about what my daughter experienced. I should not have been a disbeliever. I touched the screen with my hand and sobbed some more before I could finish my e-mails.

The next morning, I watched the orderlies and medical personnel wheel my husband into surgery and then sat alone in the quiet waiting room filled with reading material, board games and a television. The silence caused a bit of a problem for me. I was in a hospital and I see dead people. It was overwhelming. I had to pretend I did not see them so I could focus on the surgery going on with my husband. Reeking of smoke, the old leather couch provided a resting spot and with a magazine on my chest and Bobby next to me, I fell into a deep sleep, one so peaceful I always remembered it.

The color red as vivid as blood filled my mind. In the far away distance, I saw four dark figures motioning to me. I instantly felt uncomfortable and wanted to run. Their crimson faces under pointy horns frightened me. Their teeth were sharp and their ominous expressions violent. In my dream, I screamed and asked for help. Just as I began to run, a white light burst into sight and with a stroke of lightning, it destroyed the red beings. The brilliant light actually shook me and I opened my eyes. Jumping up from the worn comfortable couch, I looked around and knew the surgery was over.

Heading out of the waiting room to recovery, I walked through the busy hallways, noticing ghostly visitors with their loved ones in the rooms of other patients. I smiled at some, but let others be as I waited for my own news from the doctor. As the young surgeon walked through the corridor looking for me, I saw his shocked expression. He was amazed at the fact I knew surgery was over, but he was also stunned at another revelation.

He sat next to me in a consultation room and said the surgery went well but a lot different than he anticipated. Pausing, he went on to say that the several pre-surgical biopsies taken a month before did not show what the lab discovered after surgery. My husband had four tumors under his arm that were definitely malignant before the operation, yet they found none that were malignant. In fact, there was no sign of cancer. My husband would be healed within a few weeks.

The doctor was actually apologetic and I wondered if he thought we would accuse him of malpractice. I gratefully thanked him and realized that the four red beings in my dream had represented the tumors and the white lightening bolt had killed the disease. I witnessed a miracle. In shock, I turned off the light in the waiting room and headed for my husband who had just beaten a deadly disease and he did not even know how it happened.

CHAPTER 26

We celebrated that health event, but over the next six years, my husband had several emergency room visits and five more critical surgeries. Additional medical expenses and a nose-diving economy drove us to near bankruptcy. Desperate, I knew I could use my gift to help us financially and by doing so, I could work at home and be with the kids. Because I had never used my psychic abilities for remuneration, I had to make sure it was the right thing to do. I used meditation and felt it would be appropriate for me to make money doing what I needed to do because the spiritual side understood I had to make a living in this lifetime. The Universe understood that I lived in an economic world. There it was.

Using the internet, I acquired a website, sent out mass e-mails and posted newsletters to a few hundred businesses. I also began to work at psychic and spiritual fairs and found it brought mass amounts of new clients. I ran the business out of my home and was booked solid for five days a week. All those readings, keeping up with the kids schedule for school, gymnastics, dance and Tae Kwon Do plus household chores and taking care of my husband, I was exhausted.

It wasn't the usual tired exhaustion. It was something else entirely. I contacted a trusted friend in the field and told her I was physically and emotionally drained. She assured me it was "Medium Exhaustion," an illness of when a Medium tends to visit the Other Side too much or simply that the medium spends too much time there and not enough in the physical world. My home business absorbed forty to sixty hours a week. My body ached. I had pains and I witnessed myself being emotionally unstable.

My psychic friend helped me with a simple prayer I used every day (sometimes several times a day) and it continued to save me from destroying myself with overwork. She gave me the guidance to get me out of the hell I felt and I don't think I could have healed from it by myself. I might have had to stop my gift entirely and that breach with the Other Side would have made the gentleman very happy.

I managed to balance life and within a year, I had built a decent clientele and debated about my web site that was no longer needed. Most of my business came by word-of-mouth. I still had the pressure of taking care of the kids, a husband who was mostly without employment, financial responsibilities and, I was trying to maintain ME. I felt myself hanging on to a thin thread that was about to let me slide down a slippery slope I could not face alone. Of course, I was never alone. I always had some poor soul around.

CHAPTER 27

"You have to help me!!" a bloodied young man in his early 20's followed me around the grocery store begging me to help him. Trying to ignore him and pick up a few things on my list as fast as I could, he popped up in front of the carriage. I would end up walking right through him. In a huff and losing my patience with this arrogant spirit, I asked what his name was.

I called him by name.

"What seems to be the problem?"

I whispered the words to him as a rather snobby well-dressed woman walked by glaring at me because it looked like I was talking to myself in the bread aisle.

"I don't know what to do! This is so confusing to me! I'm not sure where I am...I want to go home!"

My heart filled with compassion and I knew this man was lost. I knew it was of the utmost importance to find out why. I learned of how he passed in a car accident after a late night of hitting all the drinking clubs with friends, one of whom drove while intoxicated. He told me about the horror he saw on his mother's face and he questioned why he could not stay still in one spot. Totally unable to focus, he had no control over his locations and he kept popping in and out of his house. Because of his guilt, he mostly wanted to be with his parents, but if other people were in his thoughts, he would end up with them. He didn't get the concept.

"I'm always jumping around. I just want to stay in my bedroom, but I can't."

"You have to come to terms with your death," I admonished him. "You need to forgive the driver and have more discipline with your behavior," I scolded him as if I were his mother and told him he was being rude like when he approached me in the store, fencing me in and having his little temper tantrum.

He was disrespectful from the moment he knew I could see him.

"Also, you can't be walking around with your injuries any longer. You are dead. Let go and you'll begin to heal," I firmly advised with a no bull shit tone.

I knew it was difficult for him to deal with, but, grateful for my help, he left quickly as I was loading the groceries into the car. Another satisfied customer, I thought. Later that evening, he came into my living room to thank me. Blood no longer covered his head and leg and for the first time, I saw him smile. I felt hopeful because of the look on his face.

"I saw my Mom. She's still so sad. The house is exactly the same," he lamented, moving from one corner of the room to the other. Now the restlessness came mostly from just being young.

"You could spend time with her and let her sense your energy. I have a feeling she misses you so much," I said.

And, with a twinkle in his eye, he left.

I never saw him again.

He was easier than most, and I thought of the spirit of a young man I dealt with years earlier that was so difficult for me. At the time, I was not much older than he was. I found this one sitting against the painted cement block wall at the local high school where I had gone to a game. His head and sandy brown hair were covered with blood and vomit soaked the front of his shirt. As he slowly raised his head to me, the loss showed in his limpid blue eyes that held mine as I stared back at him. Jumping up and leaping to me with his young muscular legs, he began to speak regretfully.

"I didn't mean to, I swear. Please, please. You can see me...what can I do?"

He begged the question.

After running hands through his hair, he looked at his blood soaked fingers and wiped them gingerly on his pants. I could see the hole in his head where the bullet had gone through.

"I shot myself and she's going to find me and oh God...what did I do?!"

I was too shocked and disgusted to answer. Calmly turning, I began to walk away. He followed, of course, asking for help with his situation, repeating over and over what he had done. I told him I was aware of his story and I was not sure what I could do. Then, Bobby was at my side and I felt I could help this boy who had committed suicide.

"Follow me and don't say a word until I tell you to," I directed the young man. There were too many people around for me to try to communicate with him.

Heading through the rain to my vehicle, he asked no questions. Bobby, he and I sat for what seemed like hours and was probably only minutes listening to the sound of the drops hitting the roof of the car. It was my first suicide and I was not sure how to handle it. The young man was distraught and ready to take responsibility and the major problem was he did not mean to do it. He swore up and down it was an accident.

I smelled the alcohol he had consumed before he pulled the trigger and I felt his emotional distress over the loss of a girlfriend. He walked me through the scene, still fresh in his mind. It had been an evening of arguments and miscommunication involving another man. As I asked him questions, he became belligerent, acting as if I were a detective interrogating him under a witness light. He said he had used drugs and taken Jack Daniels from his father's cupboard. Under the influence of both, he took a gun from the living room closet and headed to his room. He looked in the mirror and shot himself.

I still was not sure if he meant to pull the trigger. If he looked right at his image and shot himself, quite frankly, my understanding was that he DID mean to pull the trigger. He knew exactly what he was doing even under the influence. Many times in my early life, I had been drugged or intoxicated, but part of me still knew what I was doing and I felt in control of my actions. I wanted him to take the responsibility for his actions. In a reflection of his death, he showed me the stunningly visceral vision of himself on the floor bloodied and having lost all control of body fluids. I realized that his spirit was trying to turn back the clock and not leave his body. He was in anguish, hopeless from making the wrong choice.

Bobby, the suicide victim and I sat perfectly still. Silence filled the car. A once healthy football player would now have to be on the Other Side because he had done a stupid thing. Tears fell from all of us. I reminded him that he was responsible for his actions, the behavior that affected not only him, but his friends and family. The best thing he could do now was to help them from the Other Side, but first he had to understand what he did and that it was his decision that put him where he was now.

"I am in hell for taking my own life," he spit out.

Bobby and I immediately knew that he was not in hell because Bobby was not in hell and they were in the same dimension. He would have his other chance and how lucky he was not to have gone straight to hell but to be able to live in a spiritual life. I had always heard—it was always out there—that suicides were doomed to a negative after life, but I never really believed it because I believed in the compassion of God. If a person killed himself because he was at an absolute low point in his life, to me God would not punish him for that. This was a perfect example of what I always considered was true. I walked him through all this, sort of a brief introduction on how to live after you die. He seemed to ease up a bit and realized he should be thankful for not believing all he had been told on earth.

The evening progressed. My stomach rumbled telling me I had passed the dinner hour. My suicidal client was young, handsome, talented and bright, but clung to negative emotions. Not knowing exactly how to help his suffering, he thought shooting himself was the answer. Two days after they found his body, I went to his memorial service.

Bobby was at my side. The church was filled with students and family who adored the victim and it was also filled with all the questions as to why he would kill himself. As I sat on the wooden bench, I listened to the mourners and to the deceased who were sitting with Bobby and me. The dead football player identified the people coming in for the funeral. When his girlfriend arrived, he said nothing, but popped over to her side and tried to touch her blonde curly hair. She had moved on and did not feel him at all. He realized he would never hold her again and started to cry, again realizing what he had done. Looking over at me from across the crowded room, he watched my face as I gave him a nod of "it will be okay" and I smiled to let him know he would be all right.

He popped back to me and thanked me for helping him.

"No problem," I said out loud, hoping no one would think I was talking to myself.

I walked to the closed casket and looked at the picture of the young man in cap and gown. I had not known he had just graduated and was supposed to have gone off to college. My fingers ran along the edge of the frame. It was time to go. The only one I knew in the whole place was the deceased. Bobby and I left knowing that suicidal spirits have just as much of a chance on the Other Side as anyone else. I know that for sure, especially because I have seen spirits leave the bodies of the people on life support or in comas.

Spending time with hospice patients, I have witnessed the dying process from the perspective of this world and the Other Side. Sometimes, so did the dying person. Those in the room with the patients never realized that the soul of the individual near death—in a coma, on life support or just within seconds of dying--is aware of everything that is happening. In her spirit form, one woman, who knew I was a psychic, told me that as she lay in a coma, she could hear her family fighting about what was best for her.

She visited me at my home in spirit before she was actually pronounced dead. Dressed in a floor length cream-colored silk night gown, she was perfectly made up and elegant. She looked nothing like her emaciated cancer-ridden body lying in the hospital. Upset about the disagreement among her family members, she wanted them to know that she was in pain and needed to go. She wanted her kids to let her go in peace, but the young adults stood by her bed for a solid week hoping she would awaken one more time.

The woman was able to go in and out of her body during her time in the coma and experience some life after death before she left her body completely. She stepped out of her physical self to come to me as a spirit, but she stepped back in to her body to feel the loving touches of her family. Too young to die and in denial herself, she was not ready to let go but she did not realize it.

She was a devout individual and I patiently walked her through the process of dying, I was able to give her comfort and tell her it was okay to let go. I assured her she would be at peace and would look like her former beautiful self on the Other Side. Within four hours of seeing her spirit, the word came that she had died. I could feel her smile. She was pain free.

Being with people in hospice did not distress me. I knew there was no hope for them in the physical world. Those dying had the opportunity to seek a spiritual life outside the torture of their pain ridden bodies. I sensed the spirits ready to leave. I sensed the spirits of those not sure if they should. I sensed when to intervene and when not. I just sat there with my mind conscious of my surroundings, speaking no words out loud but communicating in subconscious with the spirits.

And, I thought, blessed are we to have another chance in the after life.

CHAPTER 28

Being there for souls like the young man in the grocery store and the young football player helped me along in my career. I had found the truth for them in the confirmations. The positive reinforcement was always necessary for me to know that I was doing something good for those who had gone to the Other Side and those who had been left behind. My client number increased commensurate with the amount of people I read at the house because satisfied customers were spreading the word I was the true thing.

My husband was quite complacent about my gift by now, but the kids were maturing and I taught them more about what I did for a living. They knew that when I had appointments and they were playing in the house, they had to be quiet. They did not quite understand exactly what I was doing with those clients so one day I mentioned it to my daughter. I explained that I saw spirits of people and animals and such and the people who came over wanted to be able to find out if their loved ones were doing okay. I went on to tell her how I also helped them with other things so they might improve their lives.

Eating a banana, my daughter simply stared at me and said "So you see dead things."

Out of the mouths of babes, I thought taking her peeling off the counter and throwing it away. She said no more, washed her hands, gave me a hug and nonchalantly left the kitchen as if we had talked about the weather. The bare minimum at this juncture was enough. She accepted me and what I did. I was relieved.

I expected questions from both kids, but at this time, my son didn't seem to care or understand and our daughter just took it in stride. She knew what I did so she knew I would be receptive hearing about her visions and know exactly what she was talking about. She started to share more and more with me. I was thrilled to see her interact and know the ways of the Other Side, but I was always making sure she handled it carefully. There was good and there was evil. However, before I was able to have an in depth discussion with her on the pros and cons of being a Medium, the gentleman reared his ugly head.

One November evening, I had just returned from a long day of readings at a local Psychic Fair. I peeled off my clothes and hopping into the shower, I scrubbed my entire body, particularly for the purpose of rinsing energy I may have absorbed in the eight hours of readings. Yawning, I decided I was too tired to do the housework that could wait for the next day and I went in to kiss the kids good night. Quietly opening my daughter's door, I saw she was still awake. Sitting on the side of her bed, I kissed her forehead. Right away, I saw the look of fear on her face.

"What's wrong?" I asked, thinking she had a bad dream.

Her response stunned me to the core.

"I saw five monsters with all their insides out of their bodies."

She paused and continued to tell me that they told her that if her mother did not stop the work she was doing, they would take her away from me.

"Who said that?"

I was not sure what she was trying to tell me.

"The skeletons. They told me that they want you to stop doing what you do or they'll take me away and I don't want to go away. Please stop the readings!!"

Sitting on my lap, she cried as I assured her I would handle the situation. I made light of the whole thing to her, but I was scared out of my mind hearing what I never wanted to hear. I hugged her and told her to go back to sleep. I knew immediately what I had to do.

Still shocked, I knew right away who and what the skeletons were and under no circumstances would they haunt my children as they had me when I was a child. I knew there was a ring leader in the five evil entities, the same who haunted me when I was young. He was larger in form, always in the front with a dirty jean jacket. He had chains hanging from his waist to his pockets. The other four shadowed him in the background. It horrified and infuriated me to think they were now going after my precious children.

"Of course they would!"

I berated myself.

The battle I waged with them had gone on for years and they had only my children as a threat because they knew my kids were the most important thing in the world to me. They could not intimidate me directly, so they assumed they could get to me via my daughter and son. My husband and I vowed they would not succeed.

Within fifteen minutes of comforting my child, I went into action. Enraged to the ultimate degree, I sought assistance from a higher source. I had peace, quiet and time to meditate. Within a few short minutes, I had climbed the subconscious staircase to the place I know of as the Other Side. The response came fast.

In a darkened cold room with eyes closed and a blanket on my shivering legs, I waited to see what or who would appear to help me. As usual, I started with requests using a personal introduction, a salutation known only to me asking for my higher sources, my spirit guides. I needed their protection and reminded them they had promised to take care of my children and me if I continued doing my work. I was keeping up with my end of the bargain and needed reassurance from them that we would not lay prey—again--for the same abuse that had haunted me since I was young.

Within a few minutes and a few energy changes and with my eyes closed, I felt a sure sign of a higher presence. Unconditional love and reliance from a source I could trust was with me. Making a statement, I laid it on the line again. If I were using my gift to help others, they needed to protect us. In that instance, an angel appeared. Floating a few inches off the floor, she had long blonde curly hair framing a porcelain face. Within seconds, she disappeared, but I had my answer. She was the reminder and the confirmation of the protection we had.

Someone else was with me. I also had His attention and I asked why it should be me to endure this. I begged that another be chosen in my place, but He assured me I was the one selected because I could handle my gift. He also said I was required to teach what I knew and that it was time.

"Time for what?" I wondered, asking mostly to myself.

The response was sharp.

"What you've known all along. You are meant to teach."

I asked for information on all He wanted me to do.

"One thing at a time. Teach what you have now and the rest will come later."

In tears, I ended the meditation knowing I had to spread sage around the house again. I also had to maintain the strength not to take any crap from negative beings and to show the kids how to do the same thing. They had to know how to protect themselves. With that conclusion, I came up with the idea of starting classes for those who want to know more about the Other Side, or even learn to be intuitive themselves so they won't always have to count on someone like me. I truly felt if others knew how to do what I can do, they can simply live a more spiritual life.

Thus, I began the creation of my instructional groups.

PART FOUR
TRUTH IN KNOWLEDGE

No man can reveal to you aught but that which already lies half asleep in the dawning of your knowledge.

Kahlil Gibran: The Prophet

CHAPTER 29

Clairvoyance, Mediums, the Other Side, Crossing over the Bridge, Past Life Regression and Future Life Progression and How To Use the Law of Attraction were the titles of classes I wrote. The curricula were based on my personal experience with my gift. I taught all of them myself and knew so many things would start up around the classes. The sessions sold out every time I had them. I watched my students learn the material I shared and at times, they could see their loved ones in spirit as colors or balls of energy. They could smell them or sense them.

I loved to teach. It was making such a difference. Some, of course, did not accept the information mostly because it was not what they were looking for. Everyone came out of the classes with different perspectives. Sometimes the truth was what they did not want to hear.

Going into my classes with an open door mind helped members of the class receive knowledge one way or the other. They learned that life is not always one big rainbow and that people need to take the bad with the good and also take responsibility for both. They also learned that the subconscious mind does not lie, but always tells the truth. No one knows a person as well as the subconscious of that person. I would explain it as their gut feeling, their intuition.

Once they realized this, they started building the relationship with their guides through their subconscious where their guides dwelled and once they started trusting the answers and applying the positives they received to their lives without question, they made the necessary changes in their lives to make better decisions. I taught them that the subconscious mind of anyone knows that person better than anyone else. It is always to be trusted and once that trust is built and a person meditates with that trust, life becomes easier. Spirit guides connect by the subconscious, end of conversation, the beginning of truth.

With the cat perched on my lap, I did the best I could to answer any questions the students asked. I kept the cost at a minimum. Within a year of teaching a few classes each month, I knew I was able to facilitate most of the people who attended. I also knew that my days were becoming more and more absorbed with obligations and that something had to be relinquished. Stretched to the limit, I required more breaks in my full agenda.

Another summer had arrived when I chose to stop classes and readings until I felt I could continue them again. My decision came hard for me and for the clients who assumed they could pick up the phone or send an email asking for an appointment. I was just not available at the drop of a hat. Teachings, readings and life drained me at times and I needed to rest.

Some people were angry because I had always been at their beckon call. I enabled this by always being available to anyone. Many waited for me and I found that reassuring because I was still frustrated about my gift. I was expected to be on target constantly. I had to measure up all the time. Again, I sought guidance.

One of my female clients was a therapist and she agreed that I could use the counseling she offered. I was pleased even more to learn she was a hypnotist. Maybe this earthly advice from an earthly expert would help. Even after all the confirmations from my guides, I seemed to need more reassurance and direction about what to do in my everyday life, let alone my psychic medium life. Sharing with her would be difficult and unusual for me because I had only a few people in my inner circle.

After settling myself comfortably on the small sofa in her quaint office, I was more than ready. She counted backwards walking me through a series of steps. Already accustomed to transporting myself in and out of my subconscious and conscious, I was there in a flash. The room became hot.

I felt a bead of sweat form on my forehead as I saw my familiar large hawk. Growing louder and louder, a banging of drums came to me. I was standing absolutely naked on the green grass in my back yard. My vision-familiar hawk landed next to me and suddenly transformed to an Indian chief with long black braided hair, bronzed skin and painted face. He held the feathers of a hawk in his hands as he cleansed my body with sage. He spoke nothing as a woman joined him. Oblivious to my nakedness, she slowly walked to me. Holding a bowl of blood, she painted my face with it. Without question, I allowed her to do it.

An army of Indians began to walk out of the woods. Surrounding us and a huge fire pit, they circled to the cadence of the drums. Clouds rolled in and thunder clashed. Spinning in unison with them, I felt myself rise to the sky above the ceremony. I could not see them below me, but I could still hear the drumming. My body felt so light in its dream-like state. Like a bubble floating easily through the air, I came down to the ground landing on the carpet of soft lawn where I saw myself as a naked newborn baby resting on the earth. As the thunder and drumming grew louder, rain began to pour down and the tribe seemed to retaliate chanting their yayyayyayyay to the rhythm of the changing sky. I watched my infant self gradually mature. The tribe continued to celebrate as animals came from the forest to join us and I am now an adult.

Sunlight erupted from beneath the clouds and the Indian maid gave me her wooden bowl wanting me to drink. The same blood she had put on my face was now in my belly warming it with its satisfying taste. I watched the Chief transform back to a hawk again and with a squawk that seemed to signal the ceremony was over, he and the tribe walked back into the forest where they melded and became one with the wildlife.

I came out of the hypnosis knowing I was special and had been somehow reborn. I believed nature was relaying to me that I had to cleanse my spiritual being before continuing my life spiritually and physically. A break was necessary for me to take care of myself or I would not be able to guide the energy of those who have passed and also those who are still present. Every day, I needed to remember not to exhaust or deplete myself or I would not last long as a psychic medium or a human being. Also, my gift was required in my life to make a living. I learned to take naps when I felt drained or consumed by my gift and all the goings-on in my life and it helped me to not be consumed by what I was doing. Grateful, I knew for sure I would see this wonderful therapist again.

CHAPTER 30

One spring day, I was driving to the town hall for a typical errand when a vision clearly and vehemently materialized. My head fuzzy, I pulled over.

I drove into the parking lot of a restaurant. Walking in, I noticed a room full of people having a great time to a familiar song playing loudly from the speakers of the sound system. I crawled under the bar to access the liquor and began to serve cold beer to shouting guests. Going through the kitchen, a chef I had known for years was talking about making the Alfredo sauce. I smelled all the food, tasted the cold drink given to me and felt the dollar bills in my hand as I counted the cash at closing. The clock on the wall showed 3:30 in the morning.

Jumping from my convenient office desk, I announced that I had to go and pick up the kids.

Someone said, "I told you it wouldn't be easy."

I turned swiftly and remarked, "I never said it would be easy. I said I had to get the kids.

I left the restaurant.

My first vision into my future ended.

I found myself starting the ignition of my car and driving safely to pick up the kids. The radio blasted the same song I heard in the restaurant.

Future insights I had on behalf of other people always were clear to me but this was MY life in a vision. I found it simultaneously exciting and odd. As time passed and as I went into meditation, prayer and hypnosis, my subconscious eased into my future more frequently, probably because I was questioning where my life was leading. I believed I had the power to change whatever I chose to change. If I had what I called a red flag moment, I was cognizant of something that needed to be altered in my life.

I took the information, weighed the pros and cons and decided what would be the best avenue to take. That was what I called free will. When I read clients and saw the red flag, I alerted them to give them that opportunity.

I accepted any outcome with open arms, the good and the bad, as I had taught in my classes. I knew I was supposed to deal with the vicissitudes of life. I still had to live in the physical world. What was shown to me for my future might not have been the right path to take. I made mental notes and wrote them down because it seemed as though the visions were a part of my future, but they were not cemented in stone. My guides would advise me, like parents might do, so the decision was always mine. I could succeed or fall on my face.

Being a restaurant owner was not out of the realm of possibility and could be completely within my grasp in spite of the fact I had no funding. I knew I could trust what was being shown to me and I knew I could receive a confirmation of the vision simply by asking my guides to show me my symbol of a yellow happy face. If I received my symbol three times in a 24 hour period, the answer was yes. The restaurant would be a reality. Not knowing how I would achieve such a dream was not an issue. It was enough for me to see I was going to do it. I trusted my guides.

Within six hours, I saw my symbol on a sticker, a balloon and in the form of a ball stuck on the top of an antenna on a car on the highway. I thanked my California surfer and my Jersey boy, my dear guides, for showing me yellow smiling faces and for proving once again they had my back. I used this in my classes as a proven method to show every student, client and friend. It worked every time for me and I honored this arrangement with the spiritual world.

CHAPTER 31

Deathly ill with the flu, I had taken a rest from a weekend full of two classes, 17 readings and the typical demands of my children who wanted every spare minute I had. The business was still growing rapidly and I had very little time for anything but the spirits it seemed. There had been so many ghosts in my life over the weekend. With a long sleeve shirt and pajama pants on, I crawled into bed for a needed afternoon nap.

The thump of heavy footsteps resounded on the staircase. The rosaries that hung on the doorknobs hit the wooden doors as if someone had just entered the room quickly. I ignored the typical intrusion by a spirit. If I paid attention to the soul, I would be fully awake. I was trying to get some sleep and breathed deeply looking for that rest. Because I was already very ill, I did not have the usual physical manifestation portending danger from an evil entity. Even knowing something had entered the room, I fell asleep leaving my subconscious vulnerable.

Big mistake.

I felt a long warm breath on the skin of my face and the hissing sound of a snake next to me. Remembering a similar incident when I was a child, a feeling of pressure came upon my body working its way up from my feet to my legs, thighs and upper body. I could not breathe in my sleep and felt as if I were drowning in water.

A pulsing sensation pounded in my chest and my heart struggled to beat. In the dream, I gave up trying to breath and I saw a white light and my two uncles who drowned years before as young boys. They were now men. I was wearing my pajamas and embarrassed that I had no bra covering my large breasts. I was going to die with people seeing my boobs. I asked one of my uncles to help me. Somehow, a bra materialized on my body. I thanked him.

Then, he made like the third spirit in Charles Dickens "A Christmas Carol" and showed me what my life would be like if I were to die. We visited my daughter in school and because she was able to see spirits, she could see me and knew I was dead. I was sitting in her English class, clad in my pajama best--with my bra--and she looked at me helplessly. She asked to go to the bathroom and when she entered the girls' room, she locked the stall door behind her crying violently while hitting the door. She yelled profanity and screamed how unfair it was for me to die. I could do nothing but ask her to stop and to plead for her forgiveness.

After that shocking vision, I was taken to see my son at an older age. His blondish hair had not darkened and he had the muscular body of a gymnast. He was in a store with an adult who was helping my family because I was dead. I followed my son and whispered in his ear. He could hear me, but when he turned his head to look he did not notice anything. After failing several attempts at communication with him, I realized he was blocked and could not fully understand what he heard and felt. I knew he heard me and felt the energy of my spirit, but he just did not know what was happening. He poked around the store and he never smiled. He looked lost.

The two uncles said nothing as they returned me to my sick bed. Lying flat and deathly ill with fever, I thanked them for their time and assumed the tour to the future was a learning lesson as it had been with Scrooge. Obviously, I had to spend more time with my family and less with the Other Side. My uncles gave me a long hug and floated out the window.

I awakened with a temperature that had climbed to over 103 degrees and to several more hours of vomiting.

I looked at my daughter who lay at my side now with my malady and studied her beautiful round face and big brown eyes. I never wanted her to feel the pain she had that I witnessed in my vision. As for my son, the loss I felt from him was so strong and real that I knew I could never leave him as long as I could help it.

By this juncture in my life, I had survived a near death beating, a mini stroke due to genetic hypertension, my husband's severe maladies, financial distress due to incredible medical bills and mostly, the responsibility of my gift that was not only an occupation but sometimes a burden with all the living and dead souls with whom I lived.

Without my knowing, the tides were changing in so many different areas of the spiritual and physical life I lead. I only hoped for a safe determination of where I was heading. And, I also hoped for the guidance of any higher power to continue to help me with each season of my life.

CHAPTER 32

Winter brought a foot of fresh snow to the ground. The temperature hovered at the forty degree mark and my daughter was excited to play outside in the snow. With her pink snowsuit and her hair tied back under a lighter pink wool hat, she ventured out into the mild winter day and what should have been a great day of play.

My son was in front of the television and I grabbed the opportunity to do chores while both were occupied. Dishes were washed, laundry caught up and my pile of magazines read when I heard running footsteps up the basement stairs. I knew to be on alert for something untoward because no one would hurry up that fast unless there was an emergency. My daughter burst into the kitchen. Bright red face and wet hair, she threw herself at me hugging me and sobbing into my shirt.

She was freezing and I held her tight to warm her body and comfort her distress. In the way her 7 year old mind worked, she just blurted out the words as they came. She had seen a gentleman dressed in a black suit leaning against our garage door. She stared at him for a moment and could not catch her breath. Climbing up a snow bank, she tried to get the attention of a neighbor who was plowing his driveway. He had no clue that she was suffocating. Laughing, the gentleman watched her become blue in the face. She had nerve enough to run past him, through the garage and up the stairs to me. I heard him laugh.

She said nothing more. I knew who he was and why he was there. I reinforced the abilities her gift bestowed to her and explained that not every one can see these things and that she must keep this to herself. Again, I did not want her to become the object of suspicion or ridicule. I promised her I would take care of the man in black.

In an angry tone, I lay still on my bed and opened up my subconscious room to allow in any higher being. I waited until calmness fell over me and as soon as I thought I was able, I spilled my guts to the higher being. I was upset and disappointed that my family was being threatened once more. Just when I assumed the gentleman was out of my life, he comes back not to me, but to my daughter using her as a conduit to make me afraid.

I asked what I should do, where I should go or if I should give up the Other Side to protect my child who was so much like me that the gentleman was hunting her. He along with the forces of evil have an agenda to stop her and others like her who thwart their wrath of hurt, violence and negativity they bring into this world. The higher power reminded me that the man in black had his job. We here on earth had ours.

I had mine.

Coming out of that meditation session, I could not find words to express myself. I was upset, angry and scared to think I had to deal with this for the rest of my life. The fact that my daughter shared that onus was distressing because I knew it was always an uphill battle. Now, my son, he was entirely another special being altogether.

CHAPTER 33

"Happy birthday to you! Happy birthday to you! Happy birthd..." he sang on his bed as I walked in on him in the middle of the song. Wearing just his underwear, he turned quickly startled by my presence. Jumping off the bed and pulling the covers over his half exposed body, he cried that he didn't get to finish and that she would be mad at him.

"Who would be mad at you?" I asked.

"She would!" as he pointed a finger to the corner of his room.

Not seeing anyone there, I had to be patient questioning him for answers.

"No one is there buddy, who were you singing to? I'm not mad, just curious."

With a rub on his back to let him know I wasn't angry, he confessed.

Evidently, we had the spirit of a ten-year-old girl who spent a lot of time with the kids. She didn't want them to tell us because she thought we would ask her to leave. I asked each of the kids separately what she looked like and their precise descriptions matched exactly. This information was viable and further confirmation that my son was also becoming a medium.

A few days later, trying to look my best for an appointment, I was curling my hair and putting on make up. I heard shouting from the bedroom. Minutes later, there was a pull of my hair. I spun around to see if one of the kids was the culprit, but there was no live child in the vicinity. I don't allow spirits to play such games. I have rules they must obey or out they go.

My guess was we had a ten-year-old ghost who did not like rules and assumed she could break them. Like any child, I had to discipline her as I would my own because she kept pulling my hair and I told her she had to behave or leave. With disgust and a violent temper tantrum, she slammed the door to my bedroom and pounded down the stairs. She had temper tantrums until eight o'clock that night.

Because I had kids, souls of several passed children were comfortable staying with us. We could communicate with them. I never had a problem with strange spirits being in the house as long as they respected our space as we did theirs. It certainly was not the ideal situation for everyone, but we could handle it spiritually, positively, and openly. We knew how.

When I had my first ghost actually living with me, I had to assemble all the pieces of everything I had learned from the day one and put them together to see how they fit. The puzzle solved itself showing me that living with numerous spirits can be done with mutual respect. I had learned the answers to the unknown by living with it. One needs to LEARN how to handle co-existing normally with spirits, so I decided to teach THAT paranormal concept in classes.

The response was great from the participants with regard to what they learned and what they took as advice. I decided to build my business more this way, helping the many who lived in homes occupied by poltergeists. The residents of haunted houses were afraid and the fear distracted them from their quality of life. No one with a thirty year mortgage should be afraid of living in their house. Most of the time the spirits were friendly relatives! Word went out that I could perform house blessings and investigate paranormal issues. Again, my business boomed, and again, my attempt to help the masses added to the chaos of my life.

CHAPTER 34

Investigating homes took a lot of time in travel and "reading" the house. What surprised most of the individuals who requested my services was that most of the time their house ghost would be someone familiar to them. The home was harboring the spirit who felt safe there. Sometimes the spirits were former familiar or not familiar residents. Rarely, but not impossible, a more negative spirit terrorized spaces. I handled each case with attentive concern and admiration for those who sought my help because it takes guts for anyone to admit there even is an issue.

Realizing the work I do is serious, interesting and totally ridiculous at times. I thought how special a person has to be to solve these mysteries. Fear of their ghosts or paranormal activity brought people to me and my ability to allay this fear was so rewarding in spite of the risk. As a true psychic or medium, I was always vulnerable. It was like walking into a shark tank with no protective gear. Without total understanding of proper shields, I would be a victim.

After only about a year, the business was thriving incredulously. Word was out about my abilities. I began to receive more personal criminal cases. Due to confidentiality agreements and the safety and security of the clients, I had to keep counsel and not release any information about anything going on with the crimes. I truly felt honored, frightened, loyal, subdued, gentle and fierce while working on them. I was out to help the justice system and in many instances, I did.

My world was a ball of boiling bubbles again. I had taken on too much with all my eclectic classes, readings, investigations, house blessings and psychic fairs. I had to take a hiatus. My daily posture was nearly belligerent. Simple things irritated me and made me angry. The me in me was becoming lost. Again. Even the cat bugged me, let alone my husband!

I would hide myself in the bedroom with the door closed and shades down and nothing but silence for company. Just to get a moment's peace, I had to ignore the spirits as I had in the past. My life was out of control again and the respite I needed had to be now. I constantly questioned on how I would be able to help others if I could not help myself. I lost myself in those thoughts and had my life-long debate of whether or not it was all worth it. I finally found a night of deep rest.

In a heavy sleep, I dreamed of angelic beings surrounding my bed. No one spoke but the smell of roses wafted gently under my nose while a ball of light began to shine at my feet and slowly travel up my body radiating light in its path. Unnerved, I accepted its rejuvenation as the angelic figures looked on. As the light filled my entire body, the figures put their hands on me. Warm embraces seemed to take over as love and certainty once again entered becoming one with me.

I awoke the next morning feeling as though I had experienced a healing session or a battery recharging. Bright and bushy-tailed, I was astounded by the transpiration during the night. My spirit was enlivened simply by my asking and I vowed to remember it in the future. It turned out to be the near future at my next visit to the therapist.

PART FIVE
THE PAST

The past is the present, isn't it?
It's the future, too.
We all try to lie out of that but life won't let us.

Eugene O'Neill: Long Day's Journey into Night

CHAPTER 35

The hypnosis in my therapy session brought me to a large brick home from another time period of perhaps the Renaissance era, maybe 14th century.

I watched livestock and servants mill around the property until I saw a woman who physically resembled me. Her light brown curly long hair was tied back neatly and intertwined with pearls and flowers. A heavy gold and ruby necklace rested on the top of her generous breasts pushed up by her corset that was laced up over a maroon gown of the finest silk.

After gazing in a mirror, she walked to the open window over looking a horse barn that housed prize stallions. A young man with fair skin, closely shorn light hair and blue eyes bridled a horse. His muscular body rippled under the worn cloth of his deep brown britches as he prepared her horse for a ride that summer day. Walking down a steep staircase with riding hat in tow, the woman barely gave the stable boy a glance as she mounted her horse side saddle. Thanking him, she bid good bye and headed off into the heat of the morning.

Some time later, she rested her horse and sat under a tree. A handsome equestrian galloped up the hill looking for his lover. Seeing her, he urged his mount to hurry and when he reached her, he dismounted and tied is animal with hers. Kneeling down by her side, he voraciously captured her mouth without a word. Grasping her waist, he pulled her close to him hungrily as they stripped the impediments of their clothing and took each other under the warm sun.

Lying on the small couch, I came out of the hypnosis. I had felt, smelled and sensed every emotion of that scene to my inner core. I absolutely knew I had been that woman. It was the first time I had done a past life regression and my response pleased me as I realized that we on earth in the here and now may have lived before. The symbols we use communicating with guides and the law of attraction actually folded into a wonderful, inspiring experience. I wondered why everyone did not take the opportunity to enter past life regression. It was another thing I had to explore. It explained my love for the Renaissance period. I lived during that epoch in another life.

I believed the use of my subconscious and conscious mind daily, along with the ability to communicate with the dead, gave me the power to go back in time and to relish the total experience of literal time traveling when even the scientists didn't get it. I got it. My ego did, too, and it grew with the enjoyment of this experience. For certain, I would do this again. I could still feel the emotion, the passion and could still smell my past lover on my skin.

CHAPTER 36

My therapy proved to be sound and I learned to basically do it on my own. I put myself back into past lives. Selfish or not, it was effective helping my frame of mind. And, quite frankly, I enjoyed it, perhaps too much, so I tried throwing myself more into my classes. Sometimes my husband and kids would join me. Because of their high intuitiveness and outstanding sensory abilities, they blew away my regular students. They positively shined in every exercise, test and meditation, taking all I had to give.

I burst with pride at their acceptance and realized that if there were any legacy I wanted to leave my children it was for them to understand there is life after death. Actually, every member of my class did well except for only a few people who did not benefit due to the fact that they blocked any effort to open to the Other Side. They did not like and did not accept the answers they were looking for because of their negative attitudes.

Communicating with those who have passed can be done in several ways, but always with the power of intention and by using an open approach. I taught that one can be here and on the Other Side without passing away by having a strong desire to see, to feel, and mostly to help spirits by actually being with them and experiencing what they do. Within five minutes in a visualization and meditation technique, students can do this.

Loved ones here on earth most generally want to know how their dead loved ones are doing. Preconceived notions go out the window when they learn the truth. When people go to the Other Side and return, they witness a love so incredible and undeniable, that the beauty of truth and existence in them and their passed loved ones are amazingly known. Everyone needs to know how the Other Side works. I always believed that if this happened, the world would be more harmonious.

Meditation is a looking within. The more we practice it, the better we become because more and more doors open. I have always told my students that when class is over, their meditation should not be.

CHAPTER 37

My meditation turned to helping myself with a dose of past life regression I would experience in my home. I figured out how to bring myself back to a different time to explore what I wanted or really needed at any given time. It worked well.

I landed in a field of tall dry yellow grass. Noticing a small shack that looked like someone's home, I began to walk towards it. I was around 12 years old and wore a white t-shirt and blue jean shorts. My hair blew in the light wind as I cautiously made my way to the house. The windows were broken and dirty and I heard the noise of small children. Three boys ran out of the front door and I stopped in my tracks. I knew they were poor in their old clothes that did not fit and as if I were invisible, they ran through me to the field.

Someone was humming behind me and I saw a woman in her 30s who looked exactly like I did, but she had bags under her eyes and she was heavier. With a Southern accent, she yelled harshly to the three boys to come in to dinner. She handed each boy a bowl of oatmeal. They complained about the meal, but gobbled every bite. She bathed them with water she had boiled in the one room shack and scrubbed one of them so hard that he burst into tears.

"Hush now!" she said, doing the same to the other two.

After their bath, they flung their nightgowns over their heads and their mother told them a story of how men built train tracks. They soon fell asleep. The moment calm, she boiled some tea and sat in a rocking chair by the door. Humming what seemed to be a gospel tune, she knitted mittens while deep in prayer. Tears streamed down her face and she watched out the window as if waiting for someone. She wiped her face with the apron she had worn all day.

The door opened to a young tired-looking man carrying a lunch box and a large blacksmith tool. His boots were covered in soot and his once gray pants were now black. The muscles showed under his thin white shirt stained with bits of coal and blood. He was handsome with wide shoulders on a large frame, thick black hair and sun darkened skin.

And familiar.

I had seen him before.

I also felt like I had lingered in this past life too long. Emotions and pity rose in me for the family. I needed to go. The stairs creaked under my feet as I walked out the door to the field where I had landed. The woman seemed to notice me and held out her hands as to hold mine. I gave in without hesitation knowing that I would be holding my own hands in some where in time. As we joined together, I heard her say how sad she was and how she was suffering. It was a message to me in my current life. She wanted me to make something of myself, of what I wanted in life. She loved her husband very, very much, but living their life was too difficult and she cried to the Lord every night for the hardship to go away.

Hugging me tightly, she sobbed into my ears. I made a promise to her that I would not let myself end up like she did and that I would live my life to the fullest. Thanking her for her honest advice, I walked into the tall grass and home.

My face was drenched with tears when I woke up. I recognized the man in the regression dream. He was Gladiator man in all of his muscular glory. Shaken, I decided to leave that memory alone and not visit it again regardless of how badly I wanted to return to it.

I never saw him again.

CHAPTER 38

"Hello. I got your name from a newspaper. You're a medium, right? One that can talk to the dead? A friend of mine gave me your information and said he thought I'd like to speak with you."

After we talked for a long time, her sweet voice and demeanor convinced me to take her on as a client. I had hesitated a moment because she lived in another country and because my appointment book was full, but she badly needed information from the Other Side, so I acquiesced to a telephone appointment. This reading was the first over the wires.

Within only a week, we became fast friends, even when I discovered her connection to one of the world's most well-known celebrities. This woman had a driver, for goodness' sake. I could not figure out why she wanted to be very close friends with me. Almost immediately, I liked and adored her for who she was. She cared for me and my family as if we were her own. She became a grandmother figure to my kids, not having any grandchildren of her own. Childless and having little relatives of her own, she developed a bond with me and I with her. I enjoyed every minute of connecting her with the Other Side.

When her husband died in his nineties, I was devastated and surprised to be so affected. I had never met him, but because of my connection to his wife and hers with my family, we vicariously welcomed him, too, into our everyday life. We never met in person before he developed dementia and I always hoped that when the time came for him to pass, he would once again be as active as the Olympic athlete he was in his younger years.

Only a day after I knew of his death, I saw him dressed in the glory of his hospital Johnny. It was the first time we had actually met in person. I asked how he was doing and told him how happy I was to see him. I was already prepared to help him any way I could, but his sweet smile warmed my heart so much I had even more desire to help him on his after life journey. His ghost told me that he wanted to be young again. The quiet type, as he was in life, he did not say or tell me many things, but I told him he should be whatever age he chose and that it was possible. He then knew he could do it. Several days later, I spoke with his wife and there he was—a forty-year-old cute-as-the dickens husband.

It was one of the most difficult readings I ever gave to two people who obviously loved one another when they were together in this life. Their relationship was absolute devotion. I always kept myself at a distance with my clients, but for some reason, this instance was different. Because I had become so attached to both of them, I could not begin to control my emotions that day. I continued to do readings with her to keep her in touch with him.

Keeping my emotions in check wasn't easy, especially working on missing persons, private criminal cases or lost pets. I had to keep my professionalism intact regardless of whether or not the distressing energy was around me. I also had to handle these clients with a certain delicacy and sensitivity because their loss was different in terms of perpetration. Grief was grief, but injustices meant violations. I learned how to stay positive and respectful to grieving clients while setting aside the fact that I was a mother or friend or pet owner. I could not let myself be involved in their emotions or let myself feel like I would feel if I were in their place.

The walls and the shields went up to protect myself from the truth they would discover or it would manifest negatively in me when specific data came through. I could not always protect myself from the angst. So many times I wish I could have handled the vestiges left in me a lot better after a missing person or murder case. I guessed it was a clear sign that I was human in spite of my gift. There were times I would sob after interviewing the family of a victim. It was literally haunting for me. I would tuck in my kids at night knowing there were people out there who could never tuck in their kids again. I felt the hot pain of a knife stab in my sides. I endured the anguish in an act of rape in order to learn the identity of a perpetrator. I suffered through the affects of cancer and the heavy pressure and acute pain of a heart attack. It all came to me through the spirits.

However, any information I could glean in criminal cases was so important. I had to do it and it had to be one hundred percent the truth one way or the other. I had a job to do and that was to help solve the crime using my gift. These readings earned me a certain level of maturation in sensitivity not just to be a sensitive. Keeping counsel was critical as with all my clients, but if possible, even more so with criminal cases..

With military or law enforcement investigations, representatives would discreetly come to my home and they would hand me a bunch of folders that I would never open. I simply put the folder on my lap or held them close to me and information would ramble out of my mouth. They would listen and furiously write on their clipboards taking every word down as a note. We had a mutual confidentiality agreement.

When I was done, they were gone without a single social amenity.

Strictly business.

Secret business.

It was feast or famine with them with many cases coming in at the same time or sometimes a long lag of time in between. It just depended what they needed for the case. Sometimes I felt like the old television show, Dragnet, where the one being questioned was under a bright light. It was all so perfunctory with no emotion on the part of the representatives who brought me the folders.

In spite of the fact that all these cases were extremely difficult for me, I did end up mixing my empathy with the persons lost and I did the best I could do to comfort the families of the victims. I never regretted any victim case, civil, law enforcement or military. If the families needed to talk to their lost victims, I was there to comfort regardless of my discomfort because by being there for them, I could hasten the healing for everyone involved, dead or alive. It took my strong-willed energy to survive the suffocation of drowning or asphyxiation in a fire or worse. I felt like one-of-a-kind in dealing with it all-- the pain and grief. That strong-willed person was me in this life.

I knew for sure it was only one of many lives I had lived before.

PART SIX
THE FUTURE

The future is called "perhaps,"
Which is the only possible thing to call the future. And
the important thing is not to allow that to scare you.

Tennessee Williams: The Past, Present, and Perhaps

CHAPTER 39

Moving into future life progression was beginning to allure me on a regular basis. I sought what the universe held for me. I was supervising the lives of nearly 1500 clients, and that was just the LIVE ones. I had constant anxiety. I wanted to throw in the towel. My paranormal work consumed me with obligations for future bookings for readings, reviews of private criminal cases, teaching, paranormal investigations and house blessings. Some clients actually demanded readings.

It seemed as though my kids had endless obligations that required my attendance. I was exhausted. I had taken on more paranormal work than what was prudent. I could slow down on some appointments, but I still needed the income. I stopped many of my house calls and lost only a couple of clients but gained a bit more time for myself.

Adding to my difficulties, my personal cell phone enabled clients to contact me at all times when they were not able to reach me by e-mail or land line—my mistake in giving out the number. I appreciated the business, but, I also felt I needed some time for me and I was losing that entirely. I had no idea where I was heading and this fear of the unknown led me to use my gift to see what was in store for me. I hoped it was better than the past six years.

A chill went up my spine as I settled down to put myself into future life progression, but I had to know. I opened my mind to the future in anticipation of what was ahead for me.

I was in a large contemporary red brick dwelling. A staircase rose and curved alongside the foyer wall. The floors were dark wood and the lighting exquisite. It was a five bedroom garrison with an office that held dark cherry wood leather furniture. Books were comfortably ensconced on shelving against the wall. I walked through the house and outside to see the oversized wreaths someone was hanging. It was a very snowy December day. Wearing only my robe and slippers against the biting winter wind, I spoke to the decorator giving him directions on where to place the ornaments to coordinate with the others already in place. I noticed a frozen bird bath in the front yard.

My daughter was about 11 or 12 and gorgeous with long hair and make up. Two years younger, my son was taller than I had expected him to be at that age. I went in and cleaned up the snow on the floor. Making myself a cup of tea to ward off the outdoor chill, I stepped into a four season room filled with wicker furniture and a view of an in ground swimming pool in the back yard. I noticed a magazine in a basket and saw the date of December 2013 on the brightly colored cover. The tea warmed my throat as I drank the entire cup within minutes. Knowing I had to get ready for work and that I had a long day ahead, I headed up the curved staircase for my hot bath in an oversized tub. .

After my bath, I felt exhausted and climbed into a bed with vanilla colored linens. I fell asleep. Someone woke me a few hours later telling me I had to get up immediately or I would be late. Crying, I explained that I didn't want to go because I was too exhausted. Whoever was waiting for me could know I wasn't coming. Unfortunately, I was under contract and I had to go.

I cried as I walked into the closet filled with expensive clothing and shoes and grabbed the first thing I saw, not caring if I coordinated an outfit. My usual perfect hair and make up would cover the tear tracks because I had good practice in hiding them.

Picking me up, my driver helped me into the back seat and we drove to what seemed like forever in my mind. Neither of us spoke a word. Watching the trees and scenery go by, I sat helpless feeling I was under the control of someone else and all I was thinking about was the oversized comfortable bed that closed around me that morning.

Arriving at a studio, I was whisked away to a back stage setting. Glancing down I saw the bracelets on my wrists above perfectly manicured nails. My feet hurt in the fancy high heels as my name was called and I walked onto a stage, brushing my hair back and smiling for hundreds of strangers. Dragging myself away from thoughts of home, I started my introduction.

Coming back to the present time with my head fuzzy from that afternoon in the future, I sobbed at how lonely, tired and angry I had felt regardless of my wealth. Money did not fix what was ailing in me. I missed not having a cozy life. All the heartaches of others had gotten to me. I felt them too much. In my vision, I actually had seen myself giving up. I did not want that to happen. Again, the dilemma of helping others and what it took out of me hit home. Being a medium was so difficult under its ironical moniker of "gift" and it was taking so much out of me that I needed a break. My choice was to face the issue and force a needed respite or end up so despondent that I would give up.

I took time off and shortened my appointments. As important as my clients were to me, my sanity had to become the priority. The hats I wore personally and in my paranormal career were overwhelming with responsibilities. I had the real life people and all those on the Other Side---a never ending existence. I started writing down my experiences, especially the positive ones that went along with that existence so I could try to keep track of what I was giving out and getting in return.

CHAPTER 40

Taking notes was extremely important in this stage of my personal life and career. I truly believed I was being told secrets from a higher source on how to teach others about what I know. I had drawings made of my bridge to the Other Side. Everyone has an individual totally different bridge to cross over. I drew mine.

I even practiced my own creative source, my art work, by producing several portraits of the angelic creatures I adored the most. I framed, dated and signed and hung them when appropriate, gazing often at them to remember when a specific angel had visited or warned me of events. Usually, they came to me when I needed a reminder that I was well cared for and protected. Each spiritual visitor had the ability to heal, communicate and nurture. They were always there when I was at the lowest point in my life.

I completed art work to be part of my legacy. I wrote. I taught. When I left this world, whatever remained that was part of me would stay and grow. I knew all of us are meant to do just that. Our pet cat would sit on the drawings and leave fur on the paper as though she were giving her approval. She sat on my lap during classes and readings and was a ferocious protector hissing fiercely if any negative entity walked into the room.

She was eight years old when she lost a lot of weight. The vet told me that she was dying. Our family would be devastated without her. I know it seemed foolish to most, but she was one of us. I also knew I would see her on the Other Side and because I loved her so much, I explained the whole thing to her. For some strange reason, I knew she understood and I knew as I stroked her boney back and kissed her wet nose that her time of crossing over would be soon. It was. She passed away a few months later on Thanksgiving Day.

When we left as a family for that weekend away, I looked behind me as I closed the door and saw her little round face, green eyes and the plaintive expression on her face as she looked at me and I knew that was the last time I would see her alive. Two days later, she joined our other cat that had passed away seven years before.

Her death broke my heart because I could still see and hear her but she was on the Other Side. The kids could see her, too. Some days were emotional turmoil communicating with all the family pets that had been with us and who were now on the Other Side. It was a dichotomy of emotion. We were happy to be able to talk to them, but sad wishing they had never left us.

A few months later, I was not feeling very well. I had headaches and more headaches. I was nauseated. I lost sight for moments. A physician told me to see a specialist right away. He had prescribed several different antibiotics that were not working. He thought it was a sinus infection.

Two weeks later, a surgeon whom I trusted saw me. He had a great bed side manner and I trusted him. I felt that I was in the right place. He ordered tests and a cat scan. In the follow up office visit he told me I had what looked like polyps in my sinus cavities. He asked if I had ever been in an accident. I replied no. Before I could ask why he was asking, he told me I had vestiges from a traumatic injury to the skull that left the crack marks shaped like a lightening bolt. I needed facial surgery, particularly on my nose and jaw.

He told me it looked as though I had suffered a severe blow to the face and waited for my response. I knew immediately what he was getting at. I assured him that I was not being abused at the present and that the injury had been sustained from a past relationship. He believed me and it was the first step to healing and my letting go of the severe abuse I endured years ago.

The surgery was not a walk in the park. My nose was re-broken and the polyps removed. I had splints in my nostrils for ten days. The surgeries to my jaw would have to be completed by an oral surgeon and that ended up being more difficult and painful than I could have ever imagined.

Ultimately, I had to tolerate the various stages of nine surgeries, but it brought me to terms with the emotional and physical damages of the beating I suffered at the hands of the college guy years before. I still believed it was the gentleman using my boyfriend as a vehicle to get to me. Through the years, I had continued to have nightmares about the incident.

I was on my way to health and forgiveness and the end of suffering, I hoped. It was an epiphany. The bad dreams would vanish, I thought. I was ready to move on bringing metal plates and screws inside and out of my mouth, bone grafts and all the rest of the treatments.

Mostly, I was ready to take time to heal, physically and mentally. I smiled again, regardless of how I looked and how much it hurt. I made it through the ordeal of the beating and the damage to my body and mind and now all the suffering to rehabilitate from the surgeries and procedures. That was a fact. I survived it all and I was now catapulting into a new part of my life albeit with lots of medical bills, but I was ready to live life and face anything that came my way.

I didn't expect it to be a speeding vehicle.

CHAPTER 41

Blinded by a brilliant light, I saw and felt huge purple-framed white wings suddenly wrap around me a split second before I heard the explosive boom. Just as fast, the shimmering wings released me and the bright radiance disappeared.

The smell of burned rubber and leaking oil permeated the car and assaulted my nostrils. Still gripping the steering wheel, I stared through the broken windshield feeling the frigid winter temperature bite my face and I realized another vehicle had hit me full-force and head-on.

I gave thanks three times for not being killed.

Completely unharmed, I stepped out of a total rumpled heap of metal to face the driver of the truck that had hit me.

No one stopped to help and I was no where near Heaven, but I had seen the sight of it under the wings of an angel. And, I had also seen the truth about my life flash before me.

The wreck had destroyed the front license plate I had for years. As I held the piece of metal in my hands, I was disgusted with the man who hit me. My heart pounded and I fought the urge to vomit. My sweatshirt did not protect me from the cold that started to permeate my body and my heart. I loved my car and it was gone.

Help came in the form of law enforcement with lots of questions. The other driver denied he was on his cell phone. I had no proof for the police officers as I argued that I had seen him talking on it when he ran the red light. I had seen it with my own eyes for real and as a psychic so I could describe it in every minute detail. He still denied any culpability.

Bottom line, I was on my two feet and my children still had a mother.

I had no health insurance so I refused treatment from the emergency medical team that had arrived. After dealing with all the paperwork involved in a car accident, I retrieved my personal affects from the car. Taking a plastic bag, I filled it with my cases of music disks, slips of paper, coins and miscellaneous items from every nook and cranny.

On the floor of my car lay an angel coin I picked up in San Francisco on business the previous year. Wings spread and hands clenched together, it was the confirmation to show me that angel wings had saved me from a distracted driver who could have killed me. I clenched the coin in my hand and sobbed, shaking from relief and shock that soon turned to anger and fury at the other driver who had lied.

The kids, of course, had a million questions and wanted to see the pictures of the car. Realizing I could have been killed, they cried and hugged me. Their little hands squeezing around me reminded me to be thankful and dismiss the anger that would not help. I knew that the universe and my place in it would help me get through the next 24 hours. I also knew that the accident shocked me into the reality of knowing I had to change my life. If I had perished in the accident, I would have been one of the spirits who wished they had made different choices. I survived. I was not on the Other Side and missing out by not having another chance.

I needed to live my life the way I deemed necessary, the way I wanted to live it, not the way others demanded. Watching the tow truck drive off with the wrangled metal mess that was once my beloved car, I knew that the doctors had repaired my physical impediments and that now I must repair myself and I started making life decisions right there on the spot that very day—my own decisions, not those of my husband or anyone else in my life.

CHAPTER 42

After placating the kids about the accident, I headed up the stairs and felt a spasm of pain in my back. Nine hours later, I was in the emergency room having a number of x-rays. The ER doctor told me I had a sprained back and neck, bruised ribs, significant nerve damage to my left arm and by then, my face was starting to bruise. The emotional turmoil was manifesting again. I was miserable, but over-the-counter pain killers quelled most of the discomfort and I was grateful to be alive and left with medical instructions and a better outlook. I was not doing too badly until I saw my vehicle the next day.

Signing papers to release my car to a junkyard was like permission for euthanasia. It was going off to car heaven. I asked a young man if I could have a disk that we forgot in the CD player. I told him which car was mine.

"You were the driver of that car? Really? Just wait here a minute," he said in amazement.

He came back with four other guys who all stared at me. They all told me that that they could not believe what I had lived through and they said it must have been a miracle because when they saw the wreck, they were sure the driver had been killed. Thinking the car saved my life, they said I should get another car just like it. Tearing up, I thanked them. Little did they know that my car had helped to save me, but mostly it was an angel from the universe. Their astonishment at me being alive reminded me of my new goal to reflect on my life and be happy.

I decided to not dwell on the accident. Life went on as normal with my family supporting me in the quest for a new vehicle as I healed from physical and mental bruising. They knew I was still heart broken about the death of our cat and now the death of my car. Because I was psychic,

I had a vision I would have a used white car manufactured by the same company. It took weeks of searching on line for me to sense the right one. Then all of sudden, there it was. A pearl white used car exactly as the one that was just totaled. The price was perfect. Its owner was located in the boondocks, but I knew it was THE car and on a very snowy night I went to a large barn in the middle of no where to buy it.

The minute I saw it I realized it was the car I had seen and it started up like a dream. I had to wait for paperwork before I picked it up, but soon it was mine and I was driving basically the same car over the same roads. Unfortunately, my usual easy driving was now filled with anxiety attacks. I had post traumatic stress syndrome from the crash.

Traveling through the intersection of the accident gave me literal shock waves of fright. I tried to find different ways to get the kids to school for my sanity. Driving through those fateful four corners was really the only way. With much prayer, forgiveness to the other driver and the will to want a better life, I passed that way over and over affirming to change my life. I remembered my car on the back of the tow truck, a car that could not be repaired, but I knew I could be repaired.

Again.

Meditation was one of the ways I could always do it. I was ready

CHAPTER 43

Practicing meditation had to be an every day activity to keep my conscious and subconscious mind sane. Remembering what Bobby had taught me years before, I knew I would be using this for the rest of my life. I enjoyed practicing it in the middle of the day and before I went to bed. It helped me to relax and relieve the stress. I found myself relying on the magic of the dream like state on the Other Side and having another chance to forego my physical life.

Risk or no risk, I started to gladly escaped this world to go beyond because it was more peaceful there, not necessarily that I meet someone I enjoyed being with. My arms and my heart were both open to those visits to the past and I used regression as an escape mechanism and almost like an addiction. Most of the time, my visions were delightful.

Most of the time.

I saw a woman I had seen before at a manor. She walked down a long cemented corridor and took a left into a kitchen with a huge fireplace. Servants moved about as she handed a young boy a message for the stable hand. Then, she stepped out into a dark stairwell feeling the wall for a familiar doorknob leading to a small room. Water dripped from the ceiling telling of the rain outside and her practical thoughts told her she would have to hang her gown to be dried from the rain seeping through the stones on the wall and ceiling.

Her heart pounded. He entered the room looking at her and not saying a word. Smelling like the wood fire he had just built, he came close to her and effortlessly released the mass of ringlets held by a comb. He moved away the heavy hair that fell to frame her face and kissed her deeply while untying the laces to the corset over her gown. Her breasts exposed, he gently kissed each one gently before moving behind to press his mouth behind her neck. She spun to meet his mouth, enjoying his taste as they quickly made love on a table. They gave no thought to being discovered. As usual, their time together would be furtive and brief and then each of them would return to their separate lives on the large estate.

The sound of the doorknob moving startled the two lovers and a shocked servant saw the nearly naked couple. They ran down the dark corridor holding hands knowing time was running out. The scene changed suddenly to a few months later and the woman is now rounded in pregnancy. She is dizzy and breathless from memories of stolen moments in the past, not her condition. Praying on a Bible for a safe delivery, she has no idea if her husband or lover fathered the child. She swayed forward and back with the movement of the rocker and stared out the window.

Now, another vision comes and it is a year later. Confined to a jail cell dressed in rags, no gown or jewels, she no longer was lady of the manor. Her beautiful curls were lice-ridden as she sits without food, water or servants at her beckon call. Her former lover entered with a guard and bringing, bread, butter and apples. Sad, he related that she has been imprisoned for adultery because the fair blue-eyed child she last bore had no physical resemblance to her husband or previous children who had dark hair and eyes. Her prison sentence was for life.

Hugging her for the last time, he left to vanish in the dimly lit hall. Now, turkey, potatoes and bread with butter on a silver plate sit next to a glass of red wine. She ate, knowing this is her final meal. Within moments, she fell to the dirt floor holding the wooden rosary her lover had brought with her last meal. Her husband had guaranteed it when he prepared her supper.

Coming out of my meditation, I knew that this powerful memory had been a past life. I had no doubt because of my remarkable sensitivity to every emotion and response from the woman in the vision. She was inherent within me and even knowing her fate, I took the right to call her mine.

I knew that past lives interweave with our current lives and the people with whom we relate in this lifetime. I couldn't help but wonder who the stable hand was and when I would see him again. It could be in another past life regression or he simply could walk into my life at a post office. Only the universe could know.

CHAPTER 44

I had taken a few weeks off to recuperate from the accident and to use that time to try to analyze the direction of my life. I was piecing together all of the visions, regressions and progressions of outcomes in other therapy sessions. I wanted to hopefully come up with an answer about who I was, where I was going, how to get there and why me. Bobby dropped in to see how I was doing and I appreciated the time he took with me because he had not been around much. He reminded me to take care of myself because I still had so much work to do. I knew that, but still enjoyed the Other Side more than my life most of the time. It was too hard to give up. I told Bobby that I loved being in Past Life Regression. I soon found out why.

When I walked into the restaurant, he was sitting at a table and appeared to be managing a staff meeting. I instantly recognized him as the blue-eyed man from my past regression. He stared at me to the point of my discomfort. He would not stop looking at me. I actually turned around to make sure he was watching me not someone behind me. He WAS absolutely staring at ME.

This was the man I had spoken to, made love to, lusted after and bore a child with in another lifetime. He physically looked a little different in my present life, but the way he walked, spoke, took command and control of everyone made it clear to me that he was the one I had met over and over in meditations with my hypnosis therapist.

I picked up my pizza and left.

I did not need proof from him that he was the stable hand from centuries before, but it came two weeks later when I went back to get another pizza for the kids. He was there again. He actually asked ME if I believed in past life regressions.

My circle of past and present lives was coming to a closure so I knew a new door would open for me. My job was to separate past from present and to happily accept my decisions deleting destructive and misdirected feelings from another life. It was going to be a bumpy ride. Every time I tried to get rid of past lives, some entity thwarted my attempt.

A bad entity.

CHAPTER 45

It was spring. Sipping my cup of tea, I made my way into the living room for a badly needed night of watching television in my warm pajamas. Stunned, I saw a male presence within a huge black circle of smoke reaching fifteen feet high up to the cathedral ceiling. It exuded power. I knew that the bigger the entity was, the more density it has absorbed from the destruction and harm to people on this earth. This evil was so powerful it entered my house regardless of my omnipresent intent of not having demons present in my home. I had to get it out of my house.

And fast.

I dropped the tea cup and burned my feet while screaming at him to get out.

"Get out of my house!!!!"

Arms flailing in the air, I walked to the black smoke and screamed again for him to get out. To my horror, a large BOOM crashed my ears and shook the whole house. The dark smoke disappeared and I stood silent and motionless as the mauve colored walls around me. Carefully turning around to check the room, I could still feel its presence. Grabbing the nearest cloth to clean up the spilled tea, I was shaking uncontrollably. I turned on every light and both televisions and called a friend to talk as long as I could and then I watched a movie to take my mind off this monster.

The garage door opened on one of the bays and then I heard the basement alarm as the door went up. I rose from the couch and pushed open the door at the top of the cellar stairs. Walking down slowly, I saw no one and then it hit me.

It was the gentleman.

I pushed the door opener down as fast as I could slamming both the garage bay and the inside door shut and locking it tight behind me.

Running up the stairs, I knew an evil spirit was present. Loudly, I told the entity to go to hell. I was not willing to play his game. The following day I covered the house with the essence of sage.

It made me feel safer.

CHAPTER 46

A week after the incident, I knew I was having too much difficulty staying out of the Other Side. I really liked it there. Bobby would conveniently pop up at my lowest point in the evenings alone after the kids went to bed and I would smile and glance his way. He would disappear but it was enough and maybe affirmation I was on the right track to dismiss my past regressions.

Life went on and I kept busy with the house, jobs and the activities of the kids. I had more and more readings and teaching and because of all the energy surrounding me, I would sometimes leave my psychic door open. When this happened, I radiated my own energy in huge amounts. If I were near the ocean, the waves seem to be uncontrollably strong around me, something witnessed by those present as proof. If I had many spirits in the house at one time or a very strong energy hanging around me, energy releases any way it wants.

One day I was in a local cell phone retailer. The setting was typical with traffic buzzing by the store while the hot July sun seemed to penetrate heat through the walls of windows into the showroom filled with customers.

And, with spirits.

I was thinking that maybe that was why I felt so hot. Perhaps the air conditioning was ineffective against the sunlight. My head was buzzing with the spirits mingling among the people waiting for clerks. Of course, the spirits noticed I could see them in the store and they were all over me, surrounding me and the friend who was there to help me pick out a phone. I told him I had to go.

Now.

It wasn't soon enough. Before our purchase transaction finished, I heard a huge pop. So did every person in the place. A six foot light over the product shelves had exploded and burst into flames about seven feet away from where I stood. The wires smoked and I told them to unplug the light to prevent a major fire. Perplexed, they said that they had never had a fixture burst like that. I assured them it would never happen again.

I went home and took a nap.

CHAPTER 47

Because the day had been particularly emotional and overwhelming, I needed that nap. Typically, my subconscious mind was open as I lay ready for my respite. I thought a past life vision was coming, but it usually took me up to any place by stairs or through a hall way. I went up and up into my vision.

I met a man I knew who on this day would become my lover. Wearing a bathing suit and cover up, I was walking down a slight incline to the shore of a lovely lake. Three beer-bellied older fishermen were ogling me and making snide remarks. Thinking how stupid I was to be out here alone, I nervously tried to ignore them and their comments, I saw my friend at a distance coming toward me in a boat.

Anxious to be rid of the lechers, I walked more quickly to the beach. His blue eyes fixed on my face. The sun felt warm on my skin, helping to heal away the tension that had been gathering for weeks. I tasted wine and heard soft music.

Reality slammed me pulling me back with an aching head and ankle still throbbing from a two-day old bee sting, but I fought it not wanting to leave the dream that seemed so real because of all my past life regressions. I drifted back into sleep.

He was gone and I was alone in the parking lot surrounded by woods. I was in street clothes and could hear the sound of crows warning me with their cawing cries. Running to my car as fast as I could, I unlocked the door and climbed in before the gentleman, heralded by the crows, could come. I had been promiscuous while dreaming and I knew the omnipresent diabolical gentleman was the reason. I knew the difference between dreaming and past life regressions even in my sleep. I stepped on the accelerator of the car and sped off.

Two hours later, I awoke with a new perspective. I finally admitted to myself that I loved being on the Other Side to escape my life. I loved it. I was living in my dreams and past life regressions, sometimes future ones, to escape the things I had to deal with in this life. I was starting to exist more in the fantasy world of non-existent lovers to escape and to my dismay, I realized I really did love it.

CHAPTER 48

I dreamed I was floating in a sea of clouds, my arms wrapped around a man with olive skin and dark hair who smelled of musk and sun. I could not see his face but knew it was Gladiator Man. He held me in his strong arms, but never looked into my face. Intertwined, we twirled in the light wind surrounding us. I felt the fear of losing him and I hung on tightly, but he fell from my grasp through the clouds beneath. Never to see him again, I screamed as he perished out of my sight.

The fear woke me and I felt the beads of sweat on my forehead. I arose for a busy day of getting the kids off to school, household chores, readings and errands. I had several errands to run which would be easy without the kids by my side. Going into the bank, I saw Gladiator Man across the street. I crossed and followed him into the store with the intention of confronting him and being one on one enough to get some answers. I had not seen him in eight years and now, there he was in the flesh.

I wanted to know why he was always invading my subconscious mind and why the universe was pulling me in a direction that had confused me for months, giving me an excuse to escape from the reality of my life. He was curious, too, and maybe interested enough, to talk to me.

We went into the nearby coffee shop and he asked me about my current status. I left out the part about past life regressions. It was up to me to examine and piece together any information I could find at this time. I really did not know what to do with him and his connection to my past life. I just knew I had to stop seeing him in the past so I could go on with my future. Letting go was imperative for me. I discovered I had only questions, not affection for him. I guessed that was what I needed to know.

CHAPTER 49

It was not easy facing the fact that I had not handled the trials and travails of life very well. In essence, I used past life regressions to go where no questions were asked of me, no demands made. It was my magical entertainment assuaging my exhaustion and raw frustrations. It was a place where for a brief time I could forget who I was and it was lust leading the way during those regressions. I was in my fourth decade of life and nothing had really changed over the last ten years except me.

The business continued to grow, right along with the kids becoming older and wiser in their psychic abilities. The older they became, the discussions about the Other Side became more important. They understood more each day and my prayers were that they could handle their visions and use their gifts better than I had in the past. I hoped they would make better decisions than I did balancing life and after life.

I was busy. I now felt blessed. I had to turn down students to keep the number of participants reasonable for my classes. I rationed my time as much as I could among the psychic and earthly activities on my daily agenda. I was certain and now accepted the fact that the universe meant for me to experience ghosts, death, past lives, teaching, prophecies, angels, negative entities and all the things that go along with being a psychic medium. I continued learning from them.

When my clients left, I made sure their ghosts did also. It was a solid rule to keep my life as normal as possible. My home had its own spirits. Bobby became a more permanent stay in our home, choosing to grow with my kids and maintaining the same age as they matured. He went to school with them, complained as they did and adjusted to new things right along with them. I hoped he would continue to be with us. I wanted him to be there to see their babies grow.

CHAPTER 50

In the past, I misused my gift and that was the reason I could not distinguish present from past from future. In retrospect, I realize that after each of my very risky travels to past or future, I always breathed a sigh of relief coming home again. The truth always lay within me waiting to grow and make me richer for it.

I still have days of exhaustion, overwork and resentment of what I do for a living. I feel as though I am being pulled in different directions. I now know my truth and the truth of hundreds of others who have confided in me. I bless my life. I fuss about my life. I can be cranky.

I am human.

And, there are days when I hardly make it out of bed because of my schedule and the energy expended with my gift, but I always remember is from a higher power.

I am human.

I continue to win the battle of good over evil and I deal with truth when my guides show me the way. I know the nastiness of the gentleman is to bring me to my knees to stop me from working with the Other Side. I am constantly aware of my fight against him and it takes every effort to make the right choices. I ask for forgiveness to any and all everyday of my life.

Because, I am human.

Only the positive forces are allowed in my house. I constantly change the light bulbs in my home because they burn out frequently. Spirits derive energy from electrical currents and there are about 100 spirits who visit daily plus our pets who have passed. Some are strangers, lots of them are children and many are family. At times, they are quite loud and I have to ask for everyone to keep it down. When I am in my bedroom with the door closed, they know it means no entry.

I still have some past regressions, but for better reasons. And, it is nice for those moments to be someone else for a change when old lives come to present. I wish everyone could do what I do and see what I see.

Ghosts knock on my door.

They always will.

ADDENDUM

On February 12, 2011, I received a call from a soft-voiced woman who wanted a reading. I scheduled her for my earliest appointment two weeks out, told her I looked forward to meeting her and headed out into the crisp winter day to do errands. I saved grocery shopping for last.

As a medium, the food market is always an adventure for me with chattering spirits who love to follow me up and down the aisles, out to my car and back home. This time, as I unpacked bags from the trunk, I smelled newly cut shavings and wood and I was inundated with the droning sound of a chain saw. As a rule, spirits hook up with me as soon as clients set appointments, so I assumed what I was sensing was connected to the prospective client who booked this morning. It is not unusual for me to experience language, touch, visions and scenarios.

This particular day, the ghost of a handsome man watched me as I put away my food. He started talking to me about his life but, gently, I encouraged him to wait for his family member to arrive so he would not use up all of his energy. I promised him he would know when she arrived and he disappeared into the wall until she drove into the yard.

Greeting her at the door, we felt an immediate mutual connection—enough to shock us both. As soon as we started the reading, expression came through with apology simmered in regret from the man's spirit who had waited patiently in silence. Love and hope came through, too, for it was time for change. Explicit memories clarified confusion. Questions asked and answered shocked the client who left her business card with me.

A week passed during which I stared at her information. The Law of Attraction came through strong with regard to my life in aspects of health, prosperity, safety, spiritual guidance and reflection. I contacted her to determine what she did for a living and was rewarded when I heard that her occupation satisfied my needs in completing a pondered project. Surprisingly, and without hesitation, she agreed to risk the undertaking of helping me write and market my biography.

One of the things she asked me was if I could conjure up a spirit. Of course, I told her. The year marked the 100th anniversary of the Titanic, a tragedy that always fascinated her. Testing, I touched reference books on her desk and immediately sensed a hopeful young man waiting on a shore for a young woman who had been on the ship. And, immediately, I closed my psychic door waiting for a time to give lost spirits the respect and justice they deserved. Taking the material home, it stayed on my dining room table until I was ready.

My very young daughter, who also has the gift, had an experience that night. She saw a young man in a soaking wet white shirt, black pants and leather boots in our bathroom. He disappeared but left a puddle on the floor. I knew where he had been.

Days later, my son, also a medium, had a nightmare in which he and many people drowned. Lost souls were trying to reach me through my children. It was time for me to write about them, time to tell of the loss of life and the ghosts live beyond the death of the Titanic—all part of my next project.

Debbie Raymond-Pinet

AFTERWORD

This book reads like fiction.

It is not.

Debbie's purpose in spilling out a profile of her life is to relay the facts as she actually sees and lives them. Her existence with the living and the dead is a sacrifice and reward. Her mission is to let people know what waits beyond this earth.

Spending a lot of time with a psychic medium was bizarre. While we worked in my office, ghosts would come in. Debbie would describe them in detail. Some I knew. Some I did not know. Spirits played with our computers, some nicely, some not. Chapters would disappear. Font styles and size were not as I had saved them. Changes would un-change. The computer tech was clueless.

Debbie and I were not.

She would assure me everything was fine. Our spirit guides were keeping us on the same wave length with each other and on the right track. Obviously, being dead does not stop some souls from helping with agendas. We had "talks" with the other spirits who were having fun at our expense. And, when sitting down to work, we needed to protect ourselves from the other entities which were not so playful.

Debbie nonchalantly accepted the presence of ghosts and I grew to accept them. They were not the only adventure during the process. Debbie would write or talk in early European vernacular, fifteenth to eighteenth century, because of her visions.

None of this was a challenge really. It was just weird. And, stunningly truthful.

Death is a truth we all have to face. Hopefully, the concept is now a bit easier.

Bonnie Meroth

ACKNOWLEDGEMENTS

I want to acknowledge both the living and the dead because to me, they are the same thing--all still alive, living in their own worlds of captivity, taking up space in my subconscious and conscious mind telling me stories and sharing secrets only they can reveal. The chance to share what I know to be true to the readers is precious to me.

I am thankful for the understanding I receive when I announce to someone that I am a psychic medium. I have understood those who do not accept my gift and learned from close friends and family to take one day at a time. And, one ghost at a time. I appreciate the reminder from those who care for me and often think of those who do not. With my family, I go on creating my life not as an illusion, but of truth that is still conveying itself day after day.

I am humbled by a woman who visited my home one very cold February evening. She took a chance with my skills. Not quite understanding what I needed, she took me by the hand—literally—and showed me what could be of this gift of mine. Together with much laughter, emotion, questions and answers, the book has become its own. I sit by the words of prediction, abuse, loss, healing, spirits and strength that summarize the life of a psychic medium.

Any higher being that has surrounded dim situations in light and walked with me through any shadows has my most precious thing I have to offer: my oath to try to the best of my ability to serve those here and on the Other Side as they would see fit.

Life has no beginning and no end.

Debbie Raymond-Pinet